Trusting God While in The Hallway

Praising God in The Storm

By

Pao Viola Mbewe

ISBN: 978-1545595626

Published in UK by RMPublishers
www.rm-pa.org

Gill

I once saw a church sign announcing a sermon entitled 'Hell in the Hallway'. Intrigued, I asked the minister what she meant by that. "You know how they're always saying, 'When God closes one door, He opens another one'? Well, no one ever talks about the hell in the hallway while you're waiting for that other door to open."

Katharine Brooks Ed.D: *The Hell in the Hallway* (2009)

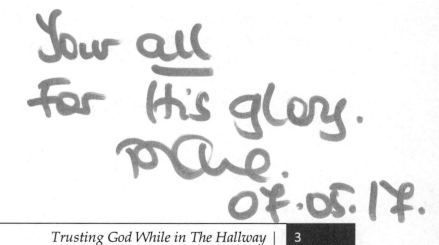

Your all
for His glory.
Dave.
07.05.17.

Trusting God While in the Hallway & Praising God in The Storm

Ministering from a Place of Pain - Bite-Sized Publications.

When you're too broken to hear clearly and listen intently, to read widely, to focus on quantity, to take another huge step to get there or you are too weighed down to reach out for help... and --

An additional 'book' is too big a task to tackle while contending with much more...

The Bite-Sized series offers snippets into victory - tools and mechanisms for coping if overwhelmed by 'perceived' complex solutions to implement... yet again.

This is an introductory book to a bite-sized series, which will expound on some chapter topics.

Dedication

The Divine connection to this assignment is purely to minister from a place of pain.

To benefit the broken-hearted, oppressed, afflicted and marginalised on a global basis.

Over and above, my own children and their descendants, God's people who have grown up carrying 'orphaned hearts' due to circumstances beyond their control or comprehension. Some of whom have suffered bereavement arising from the loss of a father, mother or core guardian as true parental figures of influence; and orphaned hearts arising from 'Absent Fathers' that were disengaged in assuming their nurturing role in owning up to a Godly responsibility to deliver His agenda.

My experience and awareness have been drawn from varied platforms. That exposure includes hearing from and observing multitudes of children and the youth; watching and hearing from friends and local communities, observations and access to information on activities within social circles, as well as factors affecting wider family and support networks.

A mother's heart for the hurting fires up a passion: (pain experienced by a woman on behalf of her offspring - as God intends). It stirred up a heart to reach out in submission to God's prompting - to open up spiritual eyes and ears. To be able to see invisible tears, hear silent cries and read the unspoken hurts from frightened faces and silenced voices, or a mere interaction... thus reading 'pain under disguise' with the intent to comfort, with the genuineness of Christ's love rather than superficial love.

The youth feature significantly as the target of this book because they form the FUTURE of this world. They are tomorrow's leaders, decision and policy makers. If they are equipped and empowered, we can expect and hope for a better tomorrow. We are investing in the future generations and progression beyond, by focusing on them now.

Some losses in personal life have ignited in the author the fire and passion for building up the broken generation. Some of these are identified in the main body - they remain present in the author's life, but God empowers her to see beyond these storms of life. One can customise this to reflect own areas of pain and distress that present as losses - and engage with tools to overcome the limitations they create in life, in the here and now. The author believes God can guide one through the journey to a place of complete healing or immense peace within the storm, hence offering clearer direction in 'doing life'.

This book attempts to equip the reader, as a resource and useful tool to help others rise above the challenges that negative situations may present.

Acknowledgements

My parents - Benson Vasco Jim and Bessie Flossie Jedegwa, for endearing love, guidance and your discipline.

Mummy, the ultimate role model - the first person I watched and admired as you relentlessly displayed the qualities and traits, of a virtuous and mighty woman of valour, in the way you executed your role as an effective mother and wife, a big sister, an Aunt, a cousin, a friend, a political figure (in the capacity of vice-chairwoman of the Women's Association - amidst numerous challenges thrown your way.

Strength, determination, the joy of the Lord, kingdom focus and a forgiving spirit describe you, the woman who raised me, through the highs and lows of life. You're extraordinary - I pray to follow in and live out that legacy - empowering my children and your future generations. Your partnership with Dad in raising us with high standards of education has impacted my life. You delivered high class...

Put simply, thank you for everything.

To Dad, for your firm ways and admirable work ethic which left nothing to be desired - a mark and a thumb-print I have been shaped to emulate. Thanks to you, I have embedded in my life discipline and self-management skills, initiative and have delivered in different settings.

You challenged me from an early age, reminding me to be a reader (with Mum keeping an eye on us there was no escape). Thank you.

To my siblings Vyson & Joe Jedegwa and Voullista Jedegwa Van Geldere

In absentia - Evelyn, Vivian, Frank, Mike, Victoria and Anthony (bless your souls).

I am who I am because of who you are and were.

I could never have achieved anything without you propelling me and lavishing me with love. I am thankful for your guidance.

To my husband, Jonathan and all our children who have believed in me. Who have seen me in study mode, when we would file 'temporary divorces' (metaphor) with each other and reconcile after submission time. Your devotion is immeasurable.

You support and cheer me on and have nursed me when I have been physically weak. For believing that I can do it when I've communicated intentions to embark on the next project or journey, to enhance my career or pursue God's calling in my life.

Spiritual giants who planted a seed, may God water the fruits of your labour:

Co-Pastor Beatrice Mwale of Hand Across Africa (Zambia) - Ladies in Fellowship Together (LIFT); for exposure to spiritual ways of God and women's fellowship and responsibility which impacted women across Gaborone, Botswana. I honour you.

Pastors Theodory John and Petronilla Elias Mlema Bandeke in Gaborone, Botswana for spiritual growth and guidance in my journey which provided a sense of safety and security around us. For continual partnership in prayer and faithfulness in feeding into my life to this date from Tanzania – Amen!

Rev Dr John Amankwatia for recognising my spiritual and human gift, and entrusting me with the responsibility as treasurer for Chesham Methodist Church. For prayer behind the scenes with wife Theresa, which kept the hinges of my faith oiled during challenges in our early years in the UK.

Reverend David and wife Jenet Jebb for the honour of working together, support work for Youth

Fellowship and behind the scenes prayers which grew my faith and reliance on God.

Residing Church Pastor and wife of TKCC - Pastor Rob and Susan Gorst. Your counsel and wisdom have brought a profound sense of freedom and self-belief in my Godly gifts. A warm atmosphere overwhelms one in the church, where displays of immeasurable love and sufficient grace are visible to all who step foot... the reflection of the Spirit of God at work is indescribable.

May God water the work of your hands and extend your territories as He continues to order your steps.

My prayer and bible study group from whom I have continued to receive support - we cannot function without each other; we share pain, joy, tears and laughter, along with a beautiful walk in the Lord.

Great encounters of significance on my journey: Botswana provided parental figures who stepped in when I needed to be 'Mothered'. Aunt and Uncle: Millie Bridget Mirriam and Captain Henry Nkosi - God-given parents in a far land stood in the comfortable distance. Life was bearable in its highs and lows because you were on hand. God's light continues to be your guide and I thank the Lord for every memory of you.

The UK saw an 'adoption' into families that embraced my family. Thank you, my mother figures: Jill McCluney and Patsy Blythe of Chesham Methodist Church. You are the reason we survived most challenges, as God planted you in my life.

Some personal friends rooted in Christ were accessible - Ann and Dick Maganga; Rose and Robert Kansichi. I acknowledge the work of Christ through you. We kept going against all odds by entrusting ourselves unto God's nurturing.

Friends and connections from high school and university years, who continue to encourage me in my walk: Cecilia, Chimwemwe, Judy and Rosemary – we draw strength from each other over the years. You have each been an instrument of God's peace in times of distress and partakers in celebratory moments.

Thank you for love that has stood the test of time, and the vote of confidence. *'I thank the Lord upon every remembrance of you'*. (Philippians 1:3)

Significant UK connections: Alan, Alex Andrew, Damien, Fiona, Gail, Marian, Pippa, Puntip and Richard. I would never have conquered some big mountains without you.

My most profound lesson exemplified by Mum remains, to work diligently as if only unto God - and I strive to emulate you:

"Whatever you do, work at it with all your heart, as working for the Lord, not for human masters," (Colossians 3:23 NIV)

"Work willingly at whatever you do, as though you were working for the Lord rather than for people." (NLT)

"Whatever you do, work heartily, as for the Lord and not for men, -" (ESV)

Lastly, my God given sisters in the UK

"One who has unreliable friends soon comes to ruin, but there is a friend who sticks closer than a brother." Proverbs 18:24 (NIV)

Nathalie Shillito – The friend that sticks closer than a brother. You have always believed in and comforted me. I have maintained sanity through the loss of Victoria and some insurmountable obstacles because you held my hand. God positioned you in my life for such a time as this. Simply – you make life bearable. I hold you in prayer today – 01.03.17.

Vonayi Nyamazana - You picked the fruit of my spirit when it was ripe and inspired me to release what was inside me, into the atmosphere. You knew the fullness of time as God used you to instigate this project. You emit extravagant love.

May God honour you in every aspect of your lives.

Most importantly,

To God be all glory.

In Jesus Christ.

Endorsements

Rob Gorst, Pastor - The Kings Church Chesham. Buckinghamshire, UK

Pao Mbewe is a beacon of light, a woman who walks the walk, and who can speak with insight and wisdom on living the overcoming life.

Despite many setbacks and complications, she has continued to pray, seek and serve in a way that is inspirational. As I began to read the book, before delving deep into it, I could see the passion with which she writes! One can sense the integrity and spiritual depth behind each sentence, and her heart to bless and inspire others.

There is a lot of energy invested in releasing her passion. I heartily recommend this book to you; the author really knows her stuff!

Finally, Pao, I want to commend you and say a big 'well done' for all the work you've put in delivering this book; it is quite an achievement! I am delighted that you proceed on this journey.

With honour and respect.

Hastings Tom Chikuse - Lay-Pastor, Influencers Church - Adelaide, Australia.

A lot has been written about victories experienced after a period of testing but not much while the testing is still in progress.

In the pages of *"Trusting God While in the Hallway"* Pao Mbewe narrates her experience of going through loss before full recovery. This book is a must read for those still in the furnace of the refiner's fire and need encouragement to keep trusting the Lord.

Cecilia Mkondiwa, MBA Vancouver, British Columbia. Canada.

Finally, a practical book that provides tools on how to operate in life by *'Trusting God While In The Hallway'*!

Sometimes this is the longest hallway one has to stand in, but Pao Mbewe has given insights on how to bridge the gap between the hallway and the exit door. The fact that the author consistently draws from her own experience and the direct and unassuming nature of her writing make this book relatable. From her daughter's walk in the hallway to her own life experiences which keep her in the hallway for a lengthy period, she shares nuggets of wisdom which we all can identify with.

A true must read for anyone who wants support as they wait on the Lord. The book offers solutions to the benefits of a receptive attitude as well as an openness to attract the Godly things….

This is a life changing book for people that feel stuck, for parents helping their children, for counsellors, the youth and simply anyone going through hardships or helping someone to get through challenging obstacles in life.

It serves as a loving hand, guiding one forward during hard times; pushing one away from own fears, while showing you where to turn and/or sit comfortably. I offer a hearty recommendation for this equipping resource.

Shadreck Chitsonga, PhD. Associate Professor of Mathematics, Fort Valley State University, USA.

'Trusting God While in The Hallway' speaks directly to the challenges of any broken-hearted individuals. The book is well crafted and offers an interesting perspective about faith and hope. The message in the book is powerful and uplifting.

Pao Viola Mbewe provides a good mix of personal experiences, analogies, and insightful quotes from the scripture that are refreshing.

I would recommend this book to any individual who wishes to engage with some survival strategies she offers. "

God's best on your journey, Pao!

Contents

Foreword

Ministering from A Place of Pain – how much would people require this resource?

Further affirmation into this mission has been drawn from insights of a virtuous woman - paraphrased herein:

Prophetic encouragement allows us to build up, cheer up and call near, as we restore Godly order and truth to the areas our enemies commonly attack. Particularly, our personhood, motives, relationships, ability and quality of work.

*"... There is no A-C, every purpose of God has a B (zone). We need to learn to minister in the B zone and not just look for the fore-telling word **but the word of immediacy.***

*Between the Calling and the Promised Land **lies the wilderness**; we are all vulnerable crossing the wilderness and need support."* (Sue Gorst, 2015)

{Excerpt: Prophetic Encouragement & the Art of Restoration – TKCC}.

Preface

This mission was borne and cultivated from personal pain, watching some close to my heart being put through avoidable pain by the selfish choices of those inflicting it - largely as a form of control, influence and power from the culprits' perspective.

As a Christian, one realises they must face, in a Christ-like manner, the challenge at hand. One must find a place of safety for the victim, as well as offer grace with forgiveness to the culprit.

I was also prompted to look beyond the world of those inflicting pain, as they would have been in their own painful lives. To give them a chance to reform meant changing their perspective by loving them. These were broken people who wouldn't know to behave any better and the Lord somewhat planted the seed for their deep need. To 'love them into wholeness' out of their brokenness which caused them to victimise others. Not an easy call and, but achievable by the grace and power of the spirit of God.

Hence, my call for outreach grows deeper, running people to a place of safety - by empowering their thinking through feasible strategies, or offering a safe haven for them to open up and face their fears - but on 'Holy ground' which germinates into prayerful habits and sharing God's truth.

My own journey into liberation was triggered by a desperate situation. oft I prayed Psalms 61:1-2 in the hope that God will not only hear but deliver the prayer as scripture declares in its entirety:

"Hear my cry, O God; Attend to my prayer.

From the end of the earth, I will cry to You,

When my heart is overwhelmed;

Lead me to the rock that is higher than I."

Because if He didn't answer promptly, the consequences were far-reaching. I was oft (and still am) on the verge of drowning. But just there, as I lose my sight... somehow, I would find His peace, wisdom and knowledge of a way out of immediate danger.

For You have been a shelter for me, A strong tower from the enemy. I will abide in Your tabernacle forever; I will trust in the shelter of Your wings (Psalms 61:3-4)

Having been taken ill in January 2013, I was confined to a couch and receiving rehabilitation therapy for management of my condition. I used the year to read more and write more - this time with not only the specific purpose of self-empowerment but also to equip me for effective preparation for links into the 'to-be' mission I sensed as God's call. Being off work, but couch-bound, in an incapacitated state made me sit still - sit in the quiet and practice more of listening in and 'hearing' from the hearts or through the eyes of others - and begin the listening journey that God had once planted as a thought. I found writing and reading therapeutic amid my pain. So, I did, with God's purpose for me.

I understood that I needed to listen NOT to voices, but RATHER with my eyes and my heart, to an aura, a touch and a feeling - at times this included a sense of smell - filth or purity in the air for instance - being symbolic and signifying difficulties or freedom respectively. I believe that God was directing me to a specific two-fold mission and I used the times of seclusion during my illnesses to seek clarity from God and strategize from His lead - on how I'd respond. The focal points came with less uncertainty and more clarity - Silent Cries and Unspoken Hurts. And then touch these individuals in God's embrace so they'd taste His goodness. The mission was to go out there (physically or virtually) to:

- See and sense 'silent cries'

- Feel and hear 'unspoken hurts'

- Release a touch and taste of God's goodness.

From the instructions, which have progressively made sense over time, I began to draft a scanty vision and broke it down to clarify what the target user would understand. This description of the purpose for the content on the online facility was designed to represent the above quest - a Facebook page was birthed whose detail is included in the epilogue.

Essence of Publication

"The Spirit itself beareth witness with our spirit, that we are the children of God: And if children, then heirs; heirs of God, and joint-heirs with Christ; if so be that we suffer with him, that we may be also glorified together..." (Romans 8:16-17)

For the past two decades, I have played a supportive role for multitudes of the youth in and around my life (family and wider social circles within local community) - by being on hand in times of dire need.

I had the intuition that God possibly used some of my connections so that I could encourage, inspire, mentor, direct, engage and most importantly; listen to people, so that He could embrace them through me.

An increasing urge to reach out to specific categories of people - particularly the youth led me to be innovative and begin to engage on a more accessible platform. My intention was to set up an operating stage, where I could embrace those who 'neither do nor need to' know me and provide them access to inspiration for living so that they can reframe their mindsets positively. Hence, equip them for times of dire need.

When raising own children, I realised that creating an equilibrium amongst varied demands and amidst parenting quest (nurturing, directing, disciplining, encouraging, motivating, mentoring, and inspiring) can be such a difficult, if not impossible, balance to strike. You are Mum, and though skilled in different areas, it is not always practical or feasible to incentivise own children to 'receive' your counsel.

I recall my early years when God began speaking to me through my own family. I'd get some responsibilities of a nurturing nature. My Dad at some point said to me 'you may think you don't need to do XYZ because you're the youngest, but remember that Joseph was the one who saved his family and the entire nation.'

This put me under slight pressure, but I soon realised that he was empowering me to be confident when I was displaced from my comfort zone. It became progressively obvious that my siblings recognised I had some form of a gift, as they oft enquired of me (despite their never-ending jokes, with the tease-line 'baby of the house, baby sister'). They sent children, or those requiring counsel, in my direction. Occasionally I'd pick up these in my interactions with the youngsters.

It has become apparent in recent years, that my own children have grown to believe in my ability to put things at ease, with friendships by bringing us together on home visits or during other runs in common interests. I am led to speak to friends or informed if someone is in distress. Through the simplest form of interaction, in a hospitable atmosphere, some felt loved and embraced for who they are, safe and comfortable. One child intimates: 'working magic is second nature to you'. Another still asks: 'Mum, why don't you start a talk show, or host something for our age group in something motivational?' etc. University life proved to adopt a similar pattern - I'd extend the generic Mum/Aunt / big sister hat to flatmates. some have drawn close enough that we could find moments for a heart-to-heart on my visits.

I shared similar interactions with close friend's children and relations of a younger age. Something enabled them to open up and I recognise now that it was God they engaged with, through me.

For a season, for a reason or for a lifetime...

Standing in as a vessel for those in difficulty, proved very rewarding, offered a sense of purpose and fulfilment, in trusting that God placed me there to accomplish His purpose and channelling His plans for their lives. in that season, for a reason - one touch, one life at a time being impacted. Part of my identity - exuding God's light, His peace, the Father's love and reflecting Jesus was a humbling experience. God values me as worthy to offer a sense of safety and security around me, as a servant.

For the past decade, my desire had been to continue engaging with the youth. In the last five years, I was losing direct links with some of these due to one daughter's progression in life. When, towards the completion of her studies, before moving on to a job, she was forced to suspend her studies (having been managing what became an 'Acute and Chronic Medical' condition - and await a turnaround).

A trigger for speaking on a virtual platform, was the optimal solution - birthing an online access page.

I pray that in engaging with the content in this book, God will begin the journey of restoration for you.

For He is the Redeemer,

In Christ.

Pao Viola Mbewe (Nee: Jedegwa)

April 2017.

Chapter 1

Peace, Be Still

You will overcome because all things work together for your good.

Our Lord Jesus Christ reminds us not to be discouraged when we go through trials, for He has also experienced these things. I am often struck by scripture in my moments of utter desperation.

Scripture in James illustrates how God identifies with our pain and somewhat cheers us on in that journey. This should teach us of God's concern over every aspect of our lives. That even as we ache, He recognises the distress we may go through. When we become too restless and begin to hear negative voices, it becomes difficult and hence potentially impossible for us to rise above the challenges presented in our path.

The obvious course of action becomes the desire to give up. Yet when we are children of God, we are equipped with the knowledge of the truth, the word of God, which we must turn to in such times to claim our promises and encourage ourselves.

In the knowledge of our suffering, James 1: 2-3 reads *'My brethren, count it all joy when you fall into various trials, knowing that the testing of your faith produces patience.'*

While in the depths of pain, scripture like this may not always instantly sound comforting as we do not immediately see a solution. However, training ourselves to believe the word and cultivate the virtue of patience, breeds a reframed mind-set which may begin to diminish the problem that we see.

Man, has the tendency to diminish all good things by self-degrading talk or undermining others. If there's a place for an undermining attitude, it is in the place of pain, problems and negativity. Those negative things MUST be belittled and counteracted.

When we hold God's viewpoint, we build the capacity to diminish the problems we experience and this propels us to engage in a fighting mode, where we can productively be on the attack in the war zone and tackle challenging situations effectively. We operate efficiently if we have clarity in our minds and hence make informed decisions.

Often, maintaining that state of mind, with correct thinking, has to be facilitated by spiritual food, hearing the word of God to deepen our faith.

Increased faith enables one to hold a positive perspective in all situations - both positive and negative. With the knowledge that God empowers us to prevail and our hope in God is always rewarded. We know this truth:

"And not only that but we also glory in tribulations, knowing that tribulation produces perseverance; - and perseverance, character; and character, hope. Now hope does not disappoint, - because the love of God has been poured out in our hearts by the Holy Spirit who was given to us." Romans 5: 3 (NKJV)

I find the gospel song by Kari Jobe 'Holy Spirit' utterly captivating as a form of worship in your broken state, as it releases one from intense pain one may be experiencing in the 'here and now', and shift one's focus to God:

The 'Holy Spirit' main verse is captivating and realigns one's focus to be set on God. From my seat, it opens up a comprehension of God's unfathomable love, while giving meaning to life's experiences 'through the rough and tough'. It presents a unique perspective from which to perceive one's struggles. Let us be encouraged to view the struggles as a set-up and stepping stone to higher ground rather than a setback. With the knowledge that God is present and carrying one through:

"I've tasted and seen, Of the sweetest of loves

Where my heart becomes free,

And my shame is undone.

Your presence, Lord.

Bridge: Holy Spirit, You are welcome here

Come flood this place and fill the atmosphere

Your glory, God, is what our hearts long for,

To be overcome by Your presence, Lord

There's nothing worth more that could ever come close. Nothing can compare,

You're our living hope,

Your presence, Lord." - Amen!

Let us hold on to this truth, as we profess our faith - that our praise to God or acknowledgement of His Supremacy is not seasonal or dependent on our personal circumstances, but rather in the knowledge that we are complete in Him.

We must confess Him as a God of all seasons, who sits on the Throne of grace in ALL seasons. Whether we hurt or not, He is on the right hand of His Father and hence we are drawn closer to remember that we have access to Him as 'He intercedes for us'. Let's believe this and act appropriately. Every challenging situation should be the perfect opportunity to give Him an offering of praise as our sacrifice and as a reminder that that's when we need Jesus to cover us in our intercession, for His glory to manifest in storms.

This knowledge then brings about peace and, a sense of stillness and calm... Despite any limitations surrounding us.

In that way, we may see the storm raging even higher around us, but we hold our peace as He calms our thoughts. At times, He calms the storm.

"Then He arose and rebuked the wind, and said to the sea, "Peace, be still!" And the wind ceased and there was a great calm." [Mark 4:39]

It takes disciplining the mind and a complete paradigm shift, to get to a place of peace; a mindset of looking beyond the storm and fixing one's gaze at the Cross of Jesus, which brings the ultimate peace. In building one's character, cultivation and nurturing any strengths requires small methodical steps into freedom. No fast-tracking and no elevator access.

Take the steps one day at a time. Be confident, calm and collected as you walk that journey, one step at a time. Trusting God to guide you. You will build a success story.

'Be still and know that I am God.' (Psalm 46:10)

Inspiration

"There is no elevator to success... You have to take the stairs." - Zig Ziglar

As hard as it may appear and as Impossible as it may seem, remember that attaining success requires earnest commitment, embedded discipline, perseverance and the investment of time.

Climbing up the ladder of success is achievable by taking a step at a time. There is no easy way up, but only strong determination.

A similar principle applies in taking on challenges in life. Stay in focus and be inspired, to overcome and earn the victory.

Peace, Be Still. Be Confident in Him, Calm & Collected.

Prayer

Father God, Abba Father

Grant me sufficient grace - grace to know you

Sufficiently, so I can Trust you

Sufficiently, so I can release myself and all to you

Sufficiently, so that I can draw inner peace

And Remind me that...

Sometimes all I need to activate a sense of Serenity...

Is to just sit at the feet of Jesus, and listen in...

Replenish inner strength and rekindle the fire;

for positive energy to enfold me

So that I can enthuse others with.

Grant me inner peace, to act & accept your word

'Peace, be still.'. Amen

Chapter 2

The Broken-Hearted and Hope

It appears that in society there is a gap in the information shared out to people, during the phase of waiting for a breakthrough or victory. We hear much about suffering, and then much about overcoming.

Yet, little appears to be spoken of about the 'in-between' journey. As one author alludes:

"No one ever talks about the hell in the hallway while you're waiting for that other door to open". (Katharine Brooks)

Some people may be like me, hearing testimonies from those who have already overcome their struggles, conquered their mountains and are now walking in victory – this is excellent as it offers an encouraging view point and is necessary for retraining the mind. How blissful that feels - to have earned freedom from lengthy perseverance and endurance. That gives me hope for tomorrow, as I sojourn.

For today though, as I fight a lengthy battle, I realise that sometimes I need more to sustain me. I need someone to hold me by the hand, to walk me through the muddy-puddle and pull me out of the mire clay that is just about to swallow me. I need someone else to help kick-start my battery which is in the vicinity of 'death' (metaphorically)... I am about to give up... it's been too long and nothing of significance seems to develop despite my personal and spiritual efforts, and endless prayer sown for various situations.

"These trials will show that your faith is genuine. It is being tested as fire tests and purifies gold --though your faith is far more precious than mere gold. So, when your faith remains strong through many trials, it will bring you much praise and glory and honour on the day when Jesus Christ is revealed to the whole world." 1 Peter 1:7 (NLT)

Expounding in a different version:

"These have come so that the proven genuineness of your faith--of greater worth than gold, which perishes even though refined by fire--may result in praise, glory and honour when Jesus Christ is revealed." NIV

The calling and relevance in this season

Obedience to a calling... 'ministering from a place of pain' - *for you are present for such a time as this… (Esther 4:14),* and I was not to be silent, not to hold my peace.

That realisation became the challenge - Do I hold my peace, in silence or act?

"For if you remain silent at this time, relief and deliverance for the Jews will arise from another place, but you and your father's family will perish. And who knows but that you have come to your royal position for such a time as this?" (NIV)

"For if thou altogether holdest thy peace at this time, then shall there enlargement and deliverance arise to the Jews from another place; but thou and thy father's house shall be destroyed: and who knoweth whether thou art come to the kingdom for such a time as this?" (KJV)

Though I do acknowledge, the fact that I'm still standing is true evidence of God at work - I have not yet shifted sufficiently to higher ground - so the affirmation I require seems to disappear. 'Where Lord... do I go?' I ask. Then I speak to Him and tune in, to listen intentionally and intently to the 'still small voice'.

Yet it's not audible enough... so I write, to Him, to myself, to my heart.

These become confessions of a distressed daughter of the Father. In distressing situations, I speak and pour my heart out. Tears oft flow as I sob or cry my heart out in loud prayer and proclamations of His word - which I desire for Him to act on and bring to pass - right in this moment.

Depiction of the Swimmer's Analogy

When someone is still 'fighting for life' by operating in survival mode as they contend, the primary aim becomes remaining afloat by implementing mechanisms to hang on in there without drowning. They may wish for active assistance to push them through the water as a 'cheerleader rather than a spectator' who has passed through and is NOW at a place of rest. They desire to know that someone identifies with them in the here and now - specifically in the desperation and fear that losing one's grip means they risk losing the fight. They need this access momentarily, to make the shore.

The cheerleader offers strategies for keeping afloat, cheering and inferring 'I am with you, we are together and I am holding your hand'.

While the spectator may implicitly sound in the striving swimmer's mind like "*Hey I did it. Earned my victories. And as you can see I'm at a place of rest. Please just focus and continue, you too will do it... Go! Go!*".

This may not accurately represent what the victor alludes, but when striving to survive, one may desire to be told 'how we do it. '*Step here, follow me - cling to my cloak, I am holding your hand...*' - as Jesus would do.

If one yearns for encouragement in this phase of '*The long walk into restoration and liberation*', then this series caters for them.

As Sue Gorst asserts:

"*We need to learn to minister in the B zone and not just look for the fore-telling word but the* **word of immediacy.**

(Prophetic) -- encouragement can help us endure the transition." -- *between the closed door and the door yet to be opened-- while in the hallway, in distress.*

Sue further presents the notion of overcoming obstacles while one is supported as she quotes Jason Vallotton:

"I have oft found myself in circumstances that were too big for me. But I've never faced anything in life that was too big for my family."

An anon author asserts:

"Whenever God opens one door, He always opens another, Even though sometimes... It's hell in the hallway." - Unknown

The Swimmer's Analogy - Unclarified Perspective

The depicted analogy presents an implicit meaning. It reflects the swimmer's subjective perception being clouded by water caught in their eyes, hence distracting their view as the head dips in and out of a raging sea. However, the victor's strategy at this stage may appear inadequate or superficial, because often victors have not narrated their *'present and active contentions - in the here and now'*. They usually share about obstacles they have already overcome.

Perhaps we could ALL learn to be more sensitive, to see the silent cries and read unspoken hurts.

I feel compelled to bridge an existing gap, by offering momentarily implementable strategies via:

o Testimonies - amid the storms

o Recognition of actively existent pain - in the here and now for those in dire need

o Strategies for Trusting God while in the hallway - phase between the storm and redemption

o Justification and benefits for praising God - while it hurts o Encouragement for 'swimmers' going against the tide to stay afloat as they battle the raging seas - anticipating their victory.

Mode - By signposting them to resources that offer strategies for walking the 'faith-talk' without faltering... though still going through the storm.

Confession - I carry immense burdens and am hence equipped and empowered to encourage others, while *I await my own restoration.*

Thus, this *resource comes from a broken vessel, for the broken world* - both perfected by God.

Because God takes the brokenness and imperfections, then mends and perfects the broken vessels into masterpieces - earthly vessels perfected and qualified for His kingdom.

We know that it's not over until God says it's over, when His work in 'perfecting' us is completed. I am testament to God's work-in-progress; I am still in a storm but I am still standing. I am still contending with trials, yet I am 'NEITHER broken NOR destroyed'.

Reason - His power works in me. When I am weak I am strong... the Bible makes '*it clear that our great power is from God, not from ourselves...*'

Thus, when God says it, that settles it, we must walk in alignment.

The Call in this book is simply to give someone hope to carry on to the next phase of their race, till they begin to see a small glimpse of light themselves, as God works through them in the same way He has worked with me.

Dr Rev Chris Oyakhilome alludes in one of his faith messages that an intercessor's responsibility is to pray and cover another for the period it takes, for the person to be able to rely on their own faith (paraphrased).

The scripture in 2 Corinthians 4 :7-9-- (NIV), not only challenges me, but also inspires me to go on, totally dependent on God's enabling power that propels me to be:

"We are hard pressed on every side, but not crushed; perplexed, but not in despair; persecuted, but not abandoned; struck down, but not destroyed."

The preceding verse, which reminds me that we always operate on God's grace and His enabling power, reads:

"But we have this treasure in jars of clay to show that this all-surpassing power is from God and not from us." NIV

The New Living Translation expounds on this as

*"We now **have this light shining in our hearts**, but we ourselves are like **fragile clay jars** containing this **great treasure**. This makes it clear that **our great power is from God, not from ourselves**..."*

The very experience of total setback and complete defeat, I felt momentarily, was the very situation that God used as a set up for this platform - where I can actively share my deepening faith and refreshed strength through trusting God, while I have been in the hallway. A time of waiting for Him to deliver me and restore my life to what I now see as a glimpse of light. To encourage one who is still hurting.

I walk through the streets and storms of pain in the here and now, but I am empowered by the completed work of the cross to help and equip others who are not yet skilled, to cope effectively.

Inspiration

The Strength of An Eagle – Rise with Wings Above the Storm.

Keep soaring above the storm, as the Lord renews your strength. (Isaiah 40:31)

Your ONLY duty is to trust Him to keep you there.

To meditate on and pray over, as need arises.

<u>Prayer - May God Give You Enough</u>

Enough strength to overcome the obstacles on your path

Sufficient grace to make your way prosperous

Spiritual eyes to see beyond the ordinary

*And **enough light for the step** you're on.*

Above all, enough confidence to know you will rise above every challenge.

Shalom!

Chapter 3

Ministering from a Place of Pain

It appears that there is an information gap in other arenas of society, some of which may be within their own geographical boundaries (physical and virtual) and others within accessible circles. Wherever that gap is, this book is intended to bridge the gap.

*"He heals the broken-hearted and **binds up their wounds**." (NIV)*

*"He heals the broken-hearted and **bandages their wounds**." (NLT)*

Points that I ponder on germinate from 'pain-full' experiences. Purpose and Passion for birthing accessible resources was germinated from a gap identified in personal needs within my surroundings.

Content accessibility can be a unique selling point due to timing. Coping mechanisms and survival Strategies are only good if they are, not only available, but also relevant in the timeline. Being applicable to the 'here and now' but also those within spiritual eye-view.

The **phase of effective outreach in brokenness lies between the storm and redemption** - it can be the longest walk. The process of walking in the long hallway of active pain and awaiting restoration can diminish hope. We possibly don't always think that those within our own vicinity or surrounding borders would be affected, or feel diminished, or can have orphaned hearts. Hence, they would find our stories accessible in that we can identify with them. Anyone on such a journey is perfect beneficiary. For they are all treasured in God's eyes, uniquely crafted in His image and set apart for His honour. Thus, offering ways of ministering to **'the broken and hurting individuals - by a broken and hurting vessel'**, in the here and now becomes relevant.

Focus is to equip people in reaching out to those equally affected, to rise above personal challenges.

The timing for the project appears to be set by God Himself, hand-picking His remnant: The Fruit is ripe, the harvest is ready, and if delayed, locusts will feed on it.

Spirit led, as there's a time for everything under earth, a season. 'He has prepared the hearts of man with receptive attitudes and teachable spirits right now' and stirred the hearts of those who desire to hear from God through someone who identifies with them in the here and now.

The Essence of Publication

The pursuit for this aspiration was ignited recently under the guidance of the Holy spirit. The fire to write material for such a platform as this had never died down - but feasibility proved unrealistic. Conversations were recently initiated, triggered by a mere enquiry on my passions.

This arose from the simplest and most ordinary of links that one would ever imagine, to which I was connected while in dire need and at a total breaking point. That link largely brought me out of the dire straits into a place of visible sanity (from my 'seat').

God has the tendency to use the ordinary and make it extraordinary; to transform the simplest men into kingdom builders. It was a kingdom builder that obeyed the voice of the holy spirit, and acted on that, which guided me through. This is evidence of supernatural intervention - as it happened within days of me pleading with God on when He would usher me onto this platform to deliver His defined mission - I was running out of time, turning fifty within three months.

I was expiring, my autopilot was cruising in the fast lane - approaching the 'sell by date'. Much faster than I could control my pedals, my meaningful life would soon be over if He didn't intervene.

Well, the intervention arrived two days after this deep communion with God, when I poured out my heart of hearts in despair about many other things. Though I still was aware that God wanted me to encourage the broken-hearted within my confines and possibly more so, the geographical setting. To reach those boundaries where the layman has no access to the Rick Warrens, Evelyn Christenson's, Derek Prince's, Mary Baxters, Benny Hinn's, Stormie Omartians, Joyce Meyers, Rod Parsleys, T.D Jakes's, Paula Whites; the Copelands (Kenneth & Gloria), The Robinsons (Betty & James), Jerry Saville's, Juanita Bynums', Helen Steiner-Rices, Zig Ziglars, Oprah Winfreys, Susan Jeffers', Paul Mckennas Mike Murdocks, Max Lucardos or Micha Jazz's of this world, in the season.

The list is endless... name every ministry I had given. God as an excuse for why 'I can't be another Author' when real effective authors are already impacting lives on His anointing.

I sensed God reminding me that the local man in my town also needs to hear His wise counsel, as will the neighbouring communities beyond my borders, without access to facilities and resources that I have been exposed to. Clarifying that perhaps I was equipped for a time such as this. If I didn't take the initiative, lives would miss out and potentially they'd be at risk.

Finally, the penny dropped! Must I cater for the local man in my neighbourhood, while the authors I listed ministered on the other operating platforms? This was the gap for the mission God presented to send me into. But I still knew I was too small for the recognition He gave me - Value and self-worth through His eyes had to be my perspective of self.

My connection with the facilitator for this mission was supernaturally **instigated**. At the initial encounter, there was the undoubted transformation from basic service delivery into a divine appointment, set up by ABBA Father in His Supremacy. One can never limit God.

Certainly, I could never anticipate the circumstances through which He will work a miracle - all these things are mysterious to us - yet we ought to have that expectancy that He will do something mind-blowing when we least expect. He can bring about transformation from a chaotic place, which mine surely was. My writing and refocusing the content I wrote to God began in the third week of January 2017. Onto this platform so I can engage with you, to give you hope. That's God's order. Divine order.

The darkest hour is indeed before dawn, but also does morning come after dawn and bring joy. (re: Provides 30:5)

We must be mindful that Jesus walked this journey too and that He remains the same Jesus, yesterday, today and forever. He is described in the bible as our 'Our Compassionate High Priest'

"Seeing then that we have a great High Priest who has passed through the heavens, Jesus the Son of God, let us hold fast our confession.

For we do not have a High Priest who cannot sympathize with our weaknesses, but was in all points tempted as we are, yet without sin. " (Hebrews 4:14-16)

We therefore have access to him, in pleading for His mercy, in our moments of distress and urgent need, where He will meet us if we earnestly pray (without losing heart and hope in God) and seek His counsel; If we present our petitions so that he may plead our cause, as He sits at the right hand of His Father. We are reminded:

"Let us therefore come boldly to the throne of grace, that we may obtain mercy and find grace to help in time of need." -- V.12

Inspiration

Your hardships are nothing to whinge over all the time.

God uses these as a set up and platform to transform you and extend His kingdom through you. How can you effectively reach out and identify... unless you've been there too; to make your story 'believable'?

Your miracle is near... the enemy only attacks those people who have a huge mission - gigantic vision.

A renowned author alludes *"Warfare often precedes the birth of a miracle."* Dr Mike Murdock

Prayer

Thank you, Abba Father, my provider, for Jesus Christ who gives us salvation and freedom

Thank you that you hold me close to your heart, in the depths of indescribable pain

And give me indescribable peace in exchange

May you keep me safe, and search my heart for any wrong that I should bring for you to cleanse

So that as I am washed, I'm purified and sanctified into righteousness

I pray that in my walk with you,

When you weigh me on your scale

I am not found wanting -- that I'm quick to repent

That I may seek to dwell in your house forever

Beholding your beauty and enquiring in your courts -

Things which you intend for the edification of my spirit, and wise counsel for my soul -- that in walking in your precepts, I shall never fail,

Nor will my faith waiver amid the highest storms.

For You promise me, that though I walk through the fire, I shall not be burned, and through the waters,

I shall not be overwhelmed. May Your promises therefore Come to pass in my life - that I physically live them as I profess my faith in You.

That I remain an effective witness of the completed work of the cross.

Father, let me be the evidence of the resurrection power of Christ - into the broken world

Where we can proclaim our position as joint-heirs of Your throne as your sons in Christ.

In Jesus' precious name. Amen.

Chapter 4

In the depths of indescribable pain

The Storm rose higher, like the first cut, with the deepest, most excruciating and paralysing pain.

No bigger, deeper, higher or greater storm has raged in my life before.

I grew up in a large family and have had some of the most beautiful experiences in my life, full of laughter, joy and contentment with many highs which resonate as I enjoy vivid recollections. This was in the midst of many lows, most of which I only learnt about in my latter years as a teenager, during university.

We have equally had a fair share of the deepest of pains one could ever imagine. I now have just three living siblings and both parents (as of March 2017 who are quite elderly), having lost six older siblings in my life.

The latest occurred six years ago, but feels as though it happened yesterday. It tore my heart for many reasons. When the person you can be yourself with, who holds the titles of **best friend, other self and 'Sister'**, goes out of physical reach, out of touch, into eternity, that creates a void. It becomes an inconceivable trauma and transforms life into such a harsh reality, that one would humanly want to run away from. The void...

Coming to terms with that reality meant I had to devise and craft personalised coping strategies, so I could continue living. Apart from suffering the effects myself, there was the added pressure (unbeknownst to me at the time) of making every necessary step to keep my children going. It became real that I was the mother figure to not only three, but six children, including hers. My mind thought and believed I had to be strong for them. More so for the three living away back at home in Malawi, as I wouldn't see or hug them every day, or at intervals (as I did with one at university away from home).

My immediate older siblings, Victoria Jean (Vicky) and Anthony Victor (Tony) and I were born three years apart. We were the youngest three in our home, while the older kids were in higher education. Hence why we were so close knit. We built a very tight friendship that was impermeable through to our married lives. I recall my brother in-law teasing me at intervals and referring to me as his 'rival' - the other person who his wife's heart belonged to. We embraced each other's spouses deeply. Such that him and my husband became very close. Tony's wife too, fitted into her slot perfectly to complete the puzzle. We three had always been inseparable.

I recall when I graduated, my brother in-law was out of employment and was soon to travel to RSA to begin as an entrepreneur. In my first job, I had access to a house where I had my sister's family move in with me. It was a two-bedroomed flat, but it made sense to share it with her and two little boys. So, I occupied the spare room with my nephews. This was the time we saw our unbreakable bond grow even stronger.

Annoyingly, to my brother in law, we would spend hours on end during nights chatting away in my bedroom, after we had finished cooking or baking. Laughing out loud and giggling. Vicky's husband would step in to either give us a telling off or 'threaten' his wife that she wasn't allowed back into the main bedroom (on a light-hearted note). We would giggle and then I'd have to detach myself to send her away to her husband, while my little nephews and my oldest niece who were also living with me, would settle into their beds.

We moved into separate homes after two years, when I got married in 1991, as I had to join my husband. This separation felt painful to me. While I was eager to move in with my new husband, the thought of not seeing my sister each evening after work and not spending weekends together did not appeal!

But we had to move on, as life determined.

Fast forwarding... After Tony slipped away into God's arms in November 2004, Vicky and I would always hold on to each other. During the funeral preparation, we went shopping for his casket, just two of us with a driver taking us places so we could pick something that would be appropriate. We thankfully found a powder blue casket, which was his favourite colour. When the feeling of loss became overwhelming at intervals, we would run off to our bedroom and cry, then wipe away the tears, praying for enough strength, then carry on with our chores and arrangements. Beyond this, we kept pulling one memory at a time, sharing the beautiful moments we experienced and laughed or cried, over years.

It was seven years later, as we begun to settle into 'life after Tony', in 2011. Suddenly, my other counterpart, the companion and soul-mate, slipped away too. I was lost. She wasn't there to share the feeling of an innermost sting, piercing deep into my heart. We didn't hold hands and run into our closet to cry together, I couldn't see, I lost sight, I lost... me, myself, lost my other self.

My world crumbled before my very eyes in an instant, yet as reality hit I realised that I couldn't run from it. Well, I wanted to and I could...

But no, I wouldn't. The circumstances surrounding my life would not allow me to run away. I have children, now six of them. Oh, they must survive this tragedy. Oh... how... how will they? How will I... how will we survive this tragedy?

I was broken - down on my knees, crushed to my bones. A strong punch hit my inner being and deep into my stomach; with hot tears and an urge to throw up... a goitre lumped up in my throat!

Yet I had to pick myself up from this mess. This complete mess had to rebuild itself to hold the hands of six young adults so they could survive through this tragedy. It was a real paralysing pain, inexplicable, unfathomable. The worst I had ever felt over the other losses of my siblings. She... was the other me. And she had been admitted into hospital at 11:00am on one January morning and had died within nine hours by 8:00pm that evening on the 9th. None of my family thought to call and alert me. All

I got was, without either warning or preparation, "Pao, we've lost Vicky"

"What? What, is this a mistake? Do you mean one of the older folk?"

As I was processing the news, I was restless. I set off as my husband spoke. I went for a run. I instantly run out of my house, uphill around my neighbourhood. We live on a steep hill, which I ran up thoughtlessly. Ran to the far end, rounded back down into main road and next to the adjacent street up hill. Heart pounding, view lost, blinded...

I didn't know where I was going, but I had to run away from this situation. It was surreal and was paralysing my heart.

No, it's not true! Immediately I rang one of my 'sons' in Malawi, I was broken.

Practically, part of me was gone. I, however, must face the world.

Yet she hadn't equipped me, as I had done with her. That realisation struck hard, stunk and was unfathomably painful. Yet, I had to cope.

Confessions of a grieving baby sister

My brother in-law, Jonas, had passed on sixteen years prior, when their kids were aged only three, five and seven, while I had a two-and-a-half-year-old and a three-month-old baby. His illness had been on and off since 1990 when he first went on a business venture to RSA. On one occasion in 1993, I had to leave my new job in Gaborone, Botswana to go nurse him in Johannesburg, as a legally recognised guardian, as he had been hospitalised as a foreigner in RSA.

This facilitated my having ample time to offer care for whatever duration. My sister and family were in Malawi. But thankfully, God always has a plan for our future. One of my closest friends had moved to Johannesburg in 1991, joining her husband and I was able to go from Gaborone a to stay with them. I was preparing meals, doing laundry and other necessities for the hospital upkeep. Staying the day with Jonas then returning home during nights, which was facilitated by the support from Rose and Steve.

My husband with our one daughter would visit on a weekend. We soon realised, when the doctors spoke to my husband (as Jonas' brother) about the severity of his condition, that we had to get my sister into the country urgently. My big brother Vyson promptly sorted out her paperwork and procured her air ticket in Malawi, while my husband and I processed Jonas's ticket and finalised the hospital formalities, arranging for emergency travel via Malawi Embassy for clearance, once he was in a stable enough state to fly back home. Jonas' condition was quite erratic, so I held back the information about Vicky's impending visit till she arrived in the ward. This pre-empted any anxiety, so that any anticipation wouldn't 'kill him' (metaphorically). His face lit up as he arose to sit up in bed, when I said I had a special present for him... his wife. We walked over to him. We were in disbelief, while deep affection was being displayed with hugs and tears shed. Jonathan and I felt we had done our job - as best as was practically possible. Our friends were a great support with resourcing us and putting us up, till the day they could fly back to Blantyre. God used them for His purpose in that season and I am ever so grateful for them.

We had my sister and husband visit Gaborone as we arranged the medical assessments and further treatment for my brother in-law; while they'd also be around to welcome my second baby for the end of

1994. Our Gaborone to Blantyre trip for Christmas visits in that year was tough. We had to stop at intervals on the way, as Jonas would intermittently have severe episodes in transit. We arrived in Blantyre safely and spent Christmas together in my parents' family home where they lived - though he was largely bed bound.

This visit was over a three-week period and I felt the impact of health on 'life'. I hurt each morning as I went to my brother in-law's guest room, adjacent to our living room, to say good morning, say hi, have a meal with him, or say bye as we got out for errands.

'Lord, he's bed bound and we can't do the normal things as we always do together, he's trapped'. I'd think, I'd hurt. I felt helpless in this situation, that I could not even exchange the hour or two with him, to carry his burden and take his place, while he took a break from his pain. No, I couldn't help him, this journey must be walked alone. My heart ached and I felt defeated.

I recall sharing this with my sister. I loved my brother in-law with a deep big-brotherly love. Being incapable of helping him this time was incomprehensibly tough.

I recognised how unfair, unjust, unreliable life could be. Suddenly, I lost trust in livelihood. He was the most beautiful soul. How did he end up here and so ill to these extents? We returned to Gaborone in January 1995.

My husband had to revisit Malawi for his sister's wedding at the end of January, so alongside preparations for the wedding, we had to organise for medication from our Doctors who treated Jonas. My parents, under whom we accessed private medical insurance, were retired and hence without facilities or resources in Malawi. Limited options were on offer. Hence imported treatment packages were crucial.

Following surgery of the stomach in the subsequent month, we unfortunately lost Jonas on February 19th, 1995.

The penny dropped. This minute as I write, I realise it's exactly 22 years ago that Jonas slipped away, in February.

Despite our attempts to help him, God had different plans. This was the hardest blow my family had ever suffered in life thus far. It was the second, after my sister Vivian's premature death, we had experienced. While Vivian had been into and out of hospital for extended periods, Jonas's illness came on suddenly and receded. On resurfacing, he rapidly went downhill after every next episode. It wasn't expected to end this way, not that soon.

This was as overwhelming for me, as it was for Vicky. Reminiscent of our journey with fine plans and then discovering we had to completely accept God's heavenly plan.

She was so broken and learnt from that point on that she only had to turn to God. The faith journey grew deeper and deeper. My family held a close embrace around my sister and the little children. Her parents providing a home for her and her big brothers offering her a business to run for her upkeep. My husband and I remained on hand for her – till her children grew up. The job was nearly done by our last visit to Malawi in summer 2009.

Suddenly, all we hoped for had lost meaning! Just when we thought we could soon relax, with her older children completing education, so that she'd enjoy the fruits of the labour over these years, she too, succumbed. I looked back at the journey. The times of taking her out of Malawi into Botswana to give her different scenery and a breather, when she was at a breaking point; to revitalise her so she was rejuvenated, with a better fighting chance to raise the kids. After all the fight, we had put up and the long difficult journey, I felt utterly conquered. We lost the war. She finally succumbed to the extreme pressure she always felt after Jonas. She gave in and I was defeated. She retreated to a simple need. She wanted to sit at the feet of her Master and rest.

I could not handle this and remain sane. I had to run away and I did just that. Run away from me, from myself, run from my life, into an 'absent zone' of my inner world.

Hence, emotional numbing became the justifiable option for my survival. To sustain the youngsters through this harsh reality, which now became our real, not imaginary, world or nightmare to wake up from; our world of pain from every possible direction we would look. My parents were distraught. She was young, only forty-six.

As intimated, the most effective strategies I had at the time have now proven futile. Everything I implemented backfired. I had to plead with God to keep me as the only living mother for the six children.

For we vowed to each other to take charge of one another's children - though in my mind it was never to be me taking up this responsibility. I had prepared her with what and how I'd want certain things 'when' I take God's call, because I would die before her. This was driven by a suspected illness that knocked on my door as I was carrying our first daughter. I had a breast cancer scare. From that point on I begun at intervals to give her memoirs and the final picture of the 'would-be' last poem or the last book/ devotional etc. I prepared her for my absence so she was sufficiently equipped. We talked through much together.

Suddenly I was physically alone.

I decided it was best to apply a mental block and operate in a somewhat absent mode, by removing and detaching my emotions. I thought it best to adopt 'emotional numbing' - the pain would be paralysed, allowing me to function.

Yes... Function. I did. Effectively? I am not sure. I became remote to myself, but I was there for the kids. Knowing myself meant acknowledging that I was 'alone' *without my precious* sister. So, it was an attractive option, to be 'at bay' with myself. I justified the imposed disconnect.

At least for a period, hopefully one year, when the children have gone *past the shock and denial*, and perhaps in the second year they would have begun the phase of *acceptance of the harsh reality*. I had it all systematically structured, at which point I would go and retrieve the pain I shelved, to start dealing with it and nurse me. Then I would reconcile to myself and pick up the pieces and embark on my grieving journey.

Well, nature would have it the natural way. This structure was not to be followed. Things went out of hand, completely, with a massive bang! A year later, I found myself ill to a point of complete debilitation.

I couldn't walk, found myself 'arrested' and trapped in my dysfunctional body, in a wheelchair a few times. What? Me? I'm always on the go, on the run, I make things happen. Lots of things depend on me to happen. What has happened?

Reality sunk in. Nearly three months into the medical investigations, there was no drawing close to diagnosing what had struck my body. The only certainty and evidence was that I was immobile and unable to even drink or feed myself. A scary reality. My children's faces and actions, made the loud statements that this was a very uncomfortable and impossible place to be in. As their dad travelled on business, they collaborated and kept things in hand, booking doctor's appointments and joining as able. It took months, brain tumour, neurological disorder and stroke were all on the plate ruled out. Phew! Much more happened.

I had to finally begin to speak about how I felt, my inner fear. Though I dreaded it, facing this without my family within reach and no support network away from home, I would possibly go into a mental breakdown and never know how to retrieve myself. Was I strong enough to bounce back? That was always the fear. Hence emotional numbing became the optimum solution for a time.

After four years, I had to acknowledge that I had implemented mal-adaptive strategies and figure out a way of un-learning what seemed to work, to re-learn functional coping strategies. I had started attending a new church - The Kings Church Chesham where I found true fellowship and relationship. Here, I was directed to church counselling service by my Pastor and his wife. I am currently receiving the support I need and my counsellor, Sally Gorton, often reminds me that even Jesus wept when He lost Lazarus and reminds me to look at scripture in the purposeful book of Lamentations. We have prayed, shared the word and she has watched lots of tears over many teas and tissues. But finally, I faced up to my fear. I was enabled by my Christian circle of those who loved and cared deeply enough. They were concerned about my welfare. The Divine Connection brought me back to a place of safety through the love, patience, and sensitivity from my Pastors Rob and Sue.

I thank God for this network and continually commit them to the Supreme Father to open floodgates of heaven, for their cause as individuals, a family, shepherds of the sheep and guides of the community of God.

For such a time as this, they were the obedient vessels, for the season.

In the last two years, I have found one Devotional Series - 'Be Still & Know' very engaging, as it has ministered to me 'from a place of pain' in the author's life. Equally, it is extremely encouraging as he constantly demonstrates in his inspirational messages, how God has walked him from his troubled place. How God shifted him from a state of brokenness into a place of utter peace. Such indescribable peace that it continues to occasionally surprise him. His walk, to me, speaks of the truth of the love of God embracing a broken man who spent years nursing his beloved wife (with MS) - with total dependence on God while seeking her healing, but to no avail. Ultimately God's plan prevailed in his life as his wife answered God's call, despite many years of sowing prayer by multitudes of people in his network.

Dr Micha Jazz expresses his 'untamed' emotions at times, which exploded in expressing his agony to God, in the immediate aftermath. He narrates on having to learn new ways of dealing with his pain, under God's teaching and guidance. Despite the hurt, he shares a journey of a deeper comprehension of God's unfathomable love, which gave him forgiveness from his anger and taught him to embrace the status-quo with God, who walked him through the loss of his wife.

His total dependence and trust has, over time grown into a genuineness of 'surrendering all' to God. He didn't realise that his act of surrendering prior to this point had been somewhat superficial. Genuineness of this act finally brought about total healing from his hurt over that loss, and what is portrayed to be 'immense peace' such that he ministers even about acceptance of death as a positive experience. Whoa!

This has been one of my few experiences of true testaments of trusting God, from my perspective, at the most vulnerable times of my life - while in the hallway. I have been ministered to and convicted even more as God has spoken many truths to me about how His presence remains. Yes, this ought to be perceived as 'tangible', but we do not see Him in those moments, because we focus our eyes more on the problem than on him, who is not only our Creator, but the Repairer of our lives which He so intricately crafted and He who knows the intricacies of our whole being.

Consequently, He is also our Problem-solver. Hence, we must be encouraged to go to Him first with any burdens, prior to taking them to other sources of support. What is apparent from these testimonials to me has been that Dr jazz has had to rely on God's truth, from the word. I noticed that as I became more dependent on 'doing life' based on the Word of God, I became richer in the knowledge of Him. In His Omniscience, ability to calm me in the storm and so began understanding more that he really is an Omniscient God who knew when I was desperate and in need. Oft I was surprised with the solutions he would usher to my direction, even if it meant to ease the pain and remove anxiety. Somehow this all-knowing God found me a solution.

Through this, God has challenged me, as this author helped me grow deeper in faith while I await my restoration, which as we speak, has not YET come to pass. I am in a position to receive and trust to witness this in 'due season'.

I am led to share the following excerpt, from the Series 'Be Still and Know', authored by Dr Micha Jazz in the hope that it will bless you:

"Prophecy and speaking in unknown languages and special knowledge will become useless. But love will last forever!". 1 Corinthians 13:8a NLT

I believe that God's love for me is never-ending. I appreciate that the decisions I need to take in response to love may not appear to be in my own self-interest. Hence, while I would like the accolade of saint for having accompanied Katey through her journey with MS, it wasn't that I didn't consider absconding when the pressure and isolation became too intense.

God hangs in with us when our attitudes, choices and behaviours may greatly disappoint him. Equally he invites us to hang in with him when his love has a strange way of revealing itself in our life's experience. I am increasingly invested in the stories of those who have endured some horrendous experience, yet have found the courage and capacity to turn this reversal into a motivation for continuing with life, and if anything, living harder.

Love which is so often presented as something of an emotion with a soft centre is in fact a solid steel backbone that affords me the opportunity to live on purpose. That purpose is God's; whose invitation is that I discover him at its very heart. My Christian life has flip-flopped on numerous occasions, yet now I see more clearly through the maturing eyes of faith that my call is simply to honour God and keep going.

I've been in some trouble with a long-standing friend, and he's withdrawn a little distance currently, because I have found myself talking positively about death. I feel as if I am on the final leg of life, and without in any way minimising the acute pain of those literally at death's door, never has life made more sense or God more real. I am excited and at peace. It's a most glorious place to be, despite the ongoing challenges of daily living."

I have intimated the experience of distress and displacement, the feeling of a complete set back and total defeat in my life for years, which has intensified in the past five to seven years as I lost my beloved sister and my daughters illness got worse and worse, followed by myself being taken ill four years ago.

The illnesses that my daughter and I face are possibly the most complex hence presenting as the biggest mountains we faced in my nuclear family. There is no known medical cure for both and as well as medically problematic to manage. Yet by the time I fell ill, I had just been through the tragedy of losing Victoria, meaning I could not share these deep emotions with her.

As I continued to care for our daughter and manage my illness, while accepting the loss of Vicky, God linked me with a service via healthcare. It was in this situation, accessing support for the very distressing experience, that God has transformed the mourning into a set up for this platform to develop - to offer support and bring joy to others.

I feel exhilarated to be able to share my deepening faith and refreshed strength through trusting God, while I have been in the hallway waiting for Him to deliver me and restore my life. And now I have begun to see it as a glimpse of light. I hope this serves as a ray of sunshine for others that are on as gloomy a journey as I have been.

I have been hesitant to write this content for others to read, because I did not think it is credible. Who would be interested in my life? Who am I, and what am I to bring something of worth and value to others? Yet on this journey, God has qualified me as He sees, as His gem. And I must see me through His lens. I am of adequate value. Because he clothes me in His grace. I am justified by grace and that qualifies me to be a worthy vessel. I must believe and accept what He offers me.

My storm remains, but I focus on the Creator and His word, by professing positively against the storm; *'to taste and see the goodness of God'* - (Psalm 34:8).

He **often** gives me peace in the midst of storms. As God gives it:

"Peace I leave with you; my peace I give you. I do not give to you as the world gives. Do not let your hearts be troubled and do not be afraid." John 14:27 (NIV)

From the pain journey, I share coping strategies. Those that failed, to ensure others guard against their adoption and the effective ones, to encourage others so that they can survive and live well in the right environment, with the right attitude and positive mind-set. By trusting God.

Further affirmation of season to release the book: The 'Fat Baby' Analogy: Rob Gorst

In one service, recently, God challenged me to look deeper internally and undertake another self-evaluation on how we release the teaching we receive - in our Christian walk. Are we growing?

The ethos of TKCC includes encouraging people from all walks of life to join the church where they will be received with open arms. One slogan reads 'Come as you are... but don't stay as you are'. In other words, do not remain there, but grow as you embrace the spiritual feed from baby milk to broth, then meat and bones; have a teachable spirit, be receptive and mature as you receive wisdom, gain knowledge and get understanding. Above all, learn to give out of your fullness.

In this sermon, he shared a vision that his wife Sue once had, where the fellowship group they belonged to, convened and communed with God over years. They grew deeper in knowledge and understanding. Yet they didn't reach out to others to share at that point. The Lord revealed to Sue that this group of spiritually filled believers were becoming too full and fat on all the spiritual food, yet wanting more without regarding the need for a release (paraphrased).

The point was, when your spirit is watered, you need to release from your belly to those who are hungry and spiritually walking in a dry season.

How comical, yet true. Ps Rob presented the challenge by posing the question - 'what good is a fat, obese baby'? - to the congregation. How profound. I gained further conviction that the book needs to be released, so I can give from the fullness of my bosom. I have had much deposited in me, but now I must equip and empower others. Off I went to complete the writing project, still unclear of the content, but relying on God to direct.

In numerous settings, Sue Gorst refers to a time when she sensed God saying that she was being 'selfish' if she didn't give out of her fullness and the knowledge of God's love, out of her filled spirit, to others who may be in need and for whom only her release would fill them. In effect, only she was the vessel God would use to answer their prayer in that season and she needed to obey to ensure she would not deprive the hungry. Otherwise, at times, the demographic setting means you are the one called to serve in that time within those boundaries.

This propelled me further into stepping back into the writing mode, to release information, if some will identify with it. Hence onto this platform, to begin the author's journey. To give out of the fullness of my belly.

Inspiration & Prayer

Faith Is a Journey... Walk It - into Greater Heights.

Release it, into an action or outreach tool.

Don't Just Sit There. Enhance it, Oil it's Hinges...

Don't settle there, Build on It.

Drop by drop, Day by day, Word by word.

Feeding one, and building another

One touch, one soul at a time.

Faith... Is A Journey, Not a Destination.

Create an overflow... as a fountain of Joy.

Deposit into your Faith account

By the word of God - enhance your account.

Withdraw from it, to water the thirsty around you.

Be empowered to tackle each day positively

Hold a perspective & an anticipation

Of ALL good things.

Every Day, Each Morning...

A Brand-New Day - with renewed mercies,

Be watered & saturated, of the Holy Spirit.

Walk the walk, and act out your faith

The 'Faith Walk'!

Agape'!   -- TCASE (Adaptation 7th Jan. '17)

Chapter 5

The Big Question to God

My approach to life had proven dysfunctional and unfortunately this only transpired following a cause-effect analysis necessary to resolve a sudden onset of an illness. It proved to be an on-going illness. Eighteen months down the line, it became clear that I had deferred dealing with my grief, possibly infinitely, running away from facing the harsh reality which I found too excruciating to confront and nurse alone.

My body had experienced severe trauma and I did nothing (or the wrong things) to help it accept and acknowledge the fact; let alone to allow it to deal with the reality and teach itself to cope in its natural ability. What I had implemented, though short term, had appeared to be to be working but was all superficial. I had suppressed my pain and operated (as though in 'pretence') in a manner that gave me visible physical normalcy and the strength to cope and maintain sanity. Internally, I was so completely torn, broken and crushed to my bones.

The shocking discovery of the onset illness, after a lengthy and painful investigative process, was that the strategies had backfired and my system was crashing. A swift overhaul was needed for my body to function again, but it was never to be a quick-fix. Everything else that happened in my life, beyond this point, was a domino effect of the mal-adaptive strategies I had adopted. A lesson learnt, may be not too late, but was late enough, as I currently must cope with a severe form of auto-immune illness which has no known medical treatment. But 'coping strategies' are given on a rehabilitation therapy programme, so much of how things go (successful or not) is dependent on what one does in self-management techniques.

My initial mechanisms had failed. Once beaten twice shy. I am doing my best to manage this, but most importantly I am trusting a good report from our Master Physician – ABBA Father to heal completely, by the resurrection power of Jesus Christ. I moved from suffering intermittent paralysis on my right side and being completely incapacitated in February - March 2013, to walking again and functioning near-normal, within five to six months by September 2013.

The team of clinicians I worked with thought it was a rapid turnaround, which they didn't normally experience, given the severity of symptoms I suffered. I was commended for persevering with the rehabilitation therapy and for retraining the brain. This was after I'd been cleared of a suspected brain tumour. In all these things, I saw God's hand, and I have faith that God has redeemed and is restoring.

The effects of these events have meant something else has had to give, while my body 'failed' to sustain itself under the trauma.

Consequently, I had to change jobs due to the illness as it impacted on my delivery. And I was unable to work full time for a period of time, while nursing myself to allow my body to rebuild itself.

I began to question God. Why this, that and the other?

As if I had not suffered enough losses, Lord...

During the illness, I felt that I had suffered the added loss of my independence at home. By this time, I had gone through a period when my two older daughters had worked together in nursing me. One occasionally came from University on Friday evening and would return on the Monday when she didn't have early morning lectures. God's mysterious intervention here was that oldest child had just undergone surgery that January (2013). And though her condition was not completely healed, the symptom alleviation in the immediate aftermath was evident (at times experienced by patients). This happened to be a season of reduction in pain levels and the fainting episodes subsequently eased.

She was out of the season for deepest need and able to be part of the support network which cared for me. God's ways are inconceivable. Another daughter maintained midweek care and at intervals the youngest would relieve her sister, if she had a break in her course work submissions - being in a crucial exam class that year. We operated effectively as enabled by God, in a spirit of solidarity, so that the mountain was broken down into hills, rocks and pebbles overtime to walk through. God's presence was at work in the situation.

The Big Question to God: WHY *are you asleep on the boat?*

The storms are rising, the waves are rough, the winds are high. There is too much going wrong and I can't talk to my sister (which we would always do with each other at every point of desperation).

Why Lord, are you asleep on the boat and not waking up to calm the storm?

I know you're the Sovereign Lord, the Creator of heaven and earth; and when you order things they obey you. So, if you say 'Peace, be still' the storm will be calm.

There was no tangible answer. I had to list all the areas of suffering. Why the illness, when I now have all the children to mother - alone? Why is the illness so complex to treat? Why do I have to be nursed? Why can't I walk yet? Why have I lost my independence? Why do I have to be lonely? Why have I lost some friends - because I don't manage the relationships anymore? And why am I experiencing the seclusion? Why can't I get up and cook for my family?

There was much interrogation directed to God and throwing tantrums as a child - to my Father in heaven. I was the untamed child in those moments. How easy it is to find many negative things in our lives, to complain about.... I got to a light bulb moment! I needed to stop complaining.

God was somewhat silent, in as far as my expectation was concerned. I felt alone.

I sat at the foot of the cross, no more words, just gazing at His radiance and waiting to be picked up. Then picking myself up and realising I needed to listen in more.

I recognised that what God had done was to calm His child, me. While the storm raged, I was finally calm amidst it.

I began to open up my spirit more readily. With an anticipation of something good, noble, pure.

The threat was that the enemy's devices were ultimately unleashed as a total attack on much of what I valued in this life. I had to change my focus and get into a battle from a different zone, my spirit.

Everything was under attack, yet one thing remained strong. The **spirit-man** and the stability of the declared truth. And so, I refocused my eyes on Jesus.

The realisation came about

In the many battles, I have fought in life and won over time, one thing EVER remained untouched. My health… until now. The domino effect of which was farther reaching and deeper cutting than I'd ever have anticipated or considered fathomable for MY life. Health » affected employment, » affected financial resources » financial stability for family » affordability of life » relationships - the list goes on.

When you're the one that often oils the hinges of relationships, the giver, the provider, a change in health is an automatic change in those relationships. An inevitable **adverse** change. Many dynamics of your life suffer negative consequences. Mine did exactly that!

Translated into further losses were my livelihood, family dynamics, functionality and my direction. Effectively, the loss of my very self. I had to learn to pick myself up from the foot of the cross, acquiring strength and giving God something of worth - myself and my time, at the feet of Jesus and a sacrifice of praise.

I often tuned into worship – words in '*I Surrender*' by Hillsong became alive to my spirit and real to my conduct, I was on my knees endlessly in brokenness:

"Here I am, down on my knees again, surrendering all;
Find me here, Lord as You draw me near; I'm desperate for you
Drench my soul, as mercy and grace unfolds; Speak to me now
Like a rushing wind, Jesus breathe within; Lord have your way in me
Like a mighty storm, stir within my soul; Lord have Your way in Me…"

His teaching in the moment of '*desolation from Him and seclusion from man*' – was piercing through my spirit. I felt comforted and enriched.

I will instruct you and teach you in the way you should go; I will counsel you with my loving eye on you. (Psalm 32:8 NIV)

Fixing my gaze on him and off the problem was a no-brainer. Other options didn't work.

This diminished the problems by magnifying Him, His power and His ability to enable me to function as though everything in my life was ok. Though beneath I was severely hurting.

His strength was activated in my action, to look away from the problem while I fixed my eyes on God, His Might to walk me through it. I walked by faith and not by sight.

In magnifying God, we create an atmosphere for God's wonders to manifest, as our actions do not intrinsically acknowledge the power of the enemy. Our actions disarm him, as we implicitly state his devices do not cause our faith to waiver; this fends off the enemy and puts him at bay.

Equally, in creating a habit of praising God, our perspective of the problems changes. We see them as 'petty inconveniences' which will bounce off 'my spirit man' as I am equipped for the battle and no arrow or dart surprises me. I have a solution for how to diffuse the attack. By a strong spiritual belief that I cannot be defeated. Simple. It's a mind-set which is not easy to adopt.

An offering of praise makes us come with a heart of worship as a sacrifice to God. I have found two songs below uplifting and reminders of where I need to be when broken --

Heart of worship and Refiner's Fire, besides the above the song:

'I'll bring you *more than a song,* for a song in itself; Is not what you have required,

You search much deeper within' – through the way things appear. You're looking into my heart

I am coming back to a heart of worship... and it's all about you, Jesus.'

Refiner's Fire - as we allow Him to purify us:

'Purify my heart, cleanse me from within and make me holy...

Purify my heart, Cleanse me from my sin... Deep within

Refiner's Fire, my heart's one desire – is to be wholly set apart for you Lord

I choose to be holy, set apart for You, my Master -- Ready to do Your will'

Inspiration by Roy Lesin - Meet Me in the Meadow

'Take His hand, even though it means letting go of what you are holding on to.

Please His heart, even though it may not please others.

Wait for His time, even though your desire is to get it done now.

Obey His Word, even though you hear something different that is popular.

Follow His path, even though you see a valley ahead.

Trust His wisdom, even though you want to do it differently.

Give Him praise, even though you are going through something unpleasant.

Be at rest, even though you have every reason to worry or fear.' Many plans are in a man's heart, But the counsel of the LORD will stand. Proverbs 19:21 NASB

Prayer for meditation: God is just a prayer away

I pray that God helps you to focus on Him

No matter what the world throws your way;

He is just a prayer away.

Remember to be kind to yourself. And

You were created in God's image and He is love,

He loves and accepts you;

He expects that in receiving His love

You will learn to love yourself, like He does.

Be kind to yourself. -- TCASE adaptation. 22/06/14

Excepts of Lyrics

The Heart of Worship - Michael W. Smith

When the music fades, All is stripped away

And I simply come, Longing just to bring

Something that's of worth, That will bless your heart

I'll bring you more than a song… For a song in itself

Is not what you have required…You search much deeper within

Through the way things appear...You're looking into my heart

I'm coming back to the heart of worship, And it's all about you,

It's all about you Jesus, I'm sorry, Lord, for the thing I've made it

When it's all about you... It's all about you, Jesus

Refiner's Fire -Brian Doerksen

Purify my heart; Let me be as gold and precious silver

Purify my heart; Let me be as gold, pure gold

Chorus:

Refiner's fire

My heart's one desire, Is to be holy

Set apart for You, Lord; I choose to be holy

Set apart for You, my Master, Ready to do Your will

[Pre-Chorus]

Purify my heart, Cleanse me from within

And make me holy, Purify my heart

Cleanse me from my sin; Deep within...

Chapter 6

Glory Comes Down

For His Glory to come down. Ministering from a place of pain, where your calling is conceived

Your most effective ministry will be birthed from a place of your deepest pain, through the refinery. So that His Kingdom comes down (on earth as it is in heaven), while you are clothed with a fragrance of grace to survive into restoration, and share testimonies.

When you have exhausted ALL options for resolve, one thing remains true, able and accessible. Dependence on God and trying Him out. You have nothing more to lose. But when all else is over and you gain your victory, you have no other person to award the credit BUT GOD.

To say, it can only be God with a sense of humility, is to overcome. Where you take all the credit and honour, and pass it straight over to God for the world to witness more of His glory.

In Your Moment of Utter Brokenness – where do you run to?

In December 2015, as I journeyed through my pain, I was reminded again to give praise to God, for His glory to come down. We don't even understand what 'His glory comes down' means. I knew a beautiful song that a worship ministry team once played on a visit to Nottingham: 'when the praises go up, His glory comes down'. This was around 2007-08.

I was aware that our unconditional and un-circumstantial joy arose and grew from a place of total release to God of our most troubling life events. But I did not fathom how this is presented to the world around us. As God continued to order my steps to teach me, I grew deeper in that knowledge.

I have had severely disheartening situations constantly going on in my life, almost each day, expecting the next attack or issue to present itself in my life, while I anticipated God to turn in and counter-act them, as the rescuer of my life.

Tommy Tenny quotes Saint Francis de Sales in one of his books – a version of *God Chasers*:

'He prays well... who is so absorbed in God that he does not know He is praying'

I have always thought this is how I want to live my life – God centred and aware.

I have learnt to generate inner peace in difficulties. I created sacred places in my house, car, office space, in my heart. I recalled years of major battle against health and another huge attack on my family and remembered how God took me to a specific place in my oldest daughter's bedroom, where I'd have a special time dedicated to God. It became My sanctuary. I prayed in all rooms of my house, and specific places like my living room, and children's bedrooms during bedtime reads and prayer time. But that bedroom was sanctified as a sanctuary. My deepest hurts and wars became easier to tackle in there. Apart from linking up with close prayer circle, there had to be a sign I had personally committed to this time to tune into God's counsel. I had an intense sense of serenity, an outpouring of God's grace and presence. This was our special meeting point, as was the **Mizpah** (Genesis 31:49 -quoted to me by Mum when I was thirteen and in boarding High School)

His glory would come down. I was affirmed that I have experienced something of His glory in the tranquillity of His presence - albeit amidst oppression.

Let's be encouraged, to be in a serene atmosphere, to create it, to build a sanctuary for God, and have an expectation of His visitation. Many battles are won there, applying discipline and keeping self-accountable to God.

Inspiration for today

Create a Sanctuary around yourself

For a true sense of Solitude

In a state of calm and serenity, find rest.

How simple this may sound

Yet it commands devotion and commitment

To the word of God, to God Himself,

And to prayer - in our brokenness.

How one responds to brokenness, has a lasting impact on where one ends up. **Succumbing to or overcoming** the critical situation at hand.

The effect of one's reciprocation or reaction to the situation, oft yielding unprecedented results or consequences. Fixing our gaze on the problem-solver, Jesus, gives us victory in spirit before we see in physical terms.

Hence this rejuvenates us to forge forward, to soldier on.

We experience His glory, for it comes down to us. Amen.

What has kept me ticking is the presence, the 'tangible' presence of God. I find myself frequently running to and resting there at the feet of Jesus, our Saviour and friend.

Just how does one tap into this invisible presence, for a sense of peace in the turbulent times? It takes personal commitment to a relationship with a redeeming God.

In there one finds beauty and solitude.

Trusting God in All Circumstances – Even When Victory Seems Unachievable.

When does one get to the point of making the conscious decision to trust completely? Is it an act imposed by circumstances? Is there no better option than tell yourself... that's it?

'I will praise God in the hallway after one door closes in waiting for the next to open'?

When does one find it of essence to 'Keep trusting and praising God while in the storm'?

And more oft than not, does one ask the question:

'Where is God when it rains?'

Well, a reflection on my recent experiences and sermons over the years, put these very questions into context, when I have not taken the word of God to mean literally what it says. I realised that in dire situations, I am challenged to partner with God, believing as I present supplications to Him, as I sow prayer in tears.

Jesus is known as a man acquainted with grief. Thus, with whose stripes we're healed. We can only trust and weep by His feet. *His ear is not too deaf to hear, nor His hand too short to deliver* (Jeremiah 32:27). We learn that God's answer comes in diverse ways as HE deems fit for our purposes. Sometimes He heals afflictions by removing the storm and other times He heals our spirit by renewing our minds. He gives us His perspective of the problem at hand and leaves the storm in our court. But we discover a tremendous amount of peace and immense levels of freedom as He liberates us from effects of the situation we face.

However God delivers His answer, we are to trust Him whole-heartedly and not over-think complexities of our mountains. Scripture says:

"Trust in the LORD with all your heart and lean not on your own understanding;"... (NIV)

Translated differently in [b] as: "...*do not depend on your own understanding.*" (NLT)

That means exactly what it says - simple, take it, believe it, behave like it and give thanks to God for His renewed mercies.

In the process of being thankful, you will recognise from news updates and other common interests how heart-breaking and heartrending events of daily life can be. Yet many of us are preserved from their impact, trauma and harm.

Which reminds us to pray for those in suffering:

"May the Lord mend hearts, emotions, organs and the spirit of the desolate and oppressed, with His miraculous touch – He encapsulates them in into the robe of righteousness; robe of Christ, that released the woman with the issue of blood from her lengthy suffering...

The same power to touch their hearts, minds and spirit so that they're made whole. Amen. "

I recall one sermon from a guest pastor who was invited in my local church to preach. His message dwelt on the challenges of a growing church.

He made a profound statement, encouraging us to '**fill the church with prayers** and **tears**, until **heaven breaks**' as he shared the story of Joshua leading the Israelites after Moses mentored him. (Billy Milton Sermon: 2015)

Fellowship in church or similar settings with believers, cultures an understanding of God's heart. We should be thankful to God for special moments in sermons, numerous testaments and scriptural highlights., to reinforce His nature and beauty as it is expressed through those fellowship circles. Such blessings given and received with love, and hearts filled with a smile.

Be reminded too, to bless these vessels, for they walk in obedience to God. To pray with compassionate hearts and take responsibility to sustain those in dire straits. And we see change in the atmosphere of our struggles. It becomes an affirmation of God hearing us when we pray. That's when His glory comes down.

Prayer - May Your Glory come down

Father God, I come to you in total surrender of my life, my needs and my broken heart as I walk through this valley of pain.

Trusting You in my journey, praising You while it hurts... for this is my testimony

That I will praise you in and out of season, because You're God in and out of season – for when my praises go up, Your glory comes down.

Father, teach me to trust you enough to surrender all, allowing me to 'die to self - my sin, pain and any inadequacies - of any form, type or manner.

And replace all that with Your tangible presence, Surrounding me with a warm embrace...

So that though I am in distress, Your peace transcends.

Meet me at my sanctuary - fill me, speak to me there.

That in my surrender, I allow you to take full control of my insurmountable obstacles,

while you clothe me in the fragrance of your grace,

Your unmerited favour given freely of Christ's death. Your never-ending love to enable, equip & empower me

That I may dwell in your house forever. Amen.

Chapter 7

Letting God by Letting Go

"To Pray is to Let go... and Let God take over!"
(Philippians 4:6-7. Adaptation mybible.com)

Scripture reminds us to trust God completely.

To have more of Him in life and less of ourselves. One, sometimes has to get to a place of desperation before they grasp this profound principle. If I allow God to run my life, 'ALL things shall be added unto me' - everything shifts into place. "But we have this treasure in earthen vessels, that the excellence of the power may be of God and not of us.")

One of the biggest challenges we face is to trust God, and doing so in *TOTAL* surrender. Which means laying the load on the cross -- and 'leaving it there' without picking it up again in the succeeding days. You may identify with this but I have on numerous occasions spoken to God, cried and thrown tantrums where I have felt that He's either too slow to come through, or indeed asleep on the boat - as the Lord did with the disciples on Galilee. I ask that He calms the storm, but occasionally when we converse I find that I'm being taught and He gives me His perspective. Which may mean 'stop worrying - it's an issue I am handling'; be strong and courageous, do not depart from the book of the law as I promise that I will never leave you. At times, I am reminded that I should have peace, not as man would give it but as God would give it. On occasion, it is simple affirmation that 'it's okay to cry, remember I experienced this too'.

I have oft experienced tremendous peace after communion with God. It's not unusual for me to go and just lay at the foot of the cross, with not words.

But a gaze on to the crucifix, where the completed work of Jesus was accomplished. Sometimes it's a deep sense of affirmation while at the feet of Jesus when He says simply - I see you, I see your tears and I love you. Are we comforted that He collects our tears?

"You number my wanderings; Put my tears into Your bottle; Are they not in Your book?" (NKJV)

You keep track of all my sorrows. You have collected all my tears in your bottle. You have recorded each one in your book. (NLT) --Psalm 56:8

I found the commentary on this verse (and chapter) on Bible hub quite enlightening - and thought, if we put this into consideration, we may begin to practice our faith differently. In bold are some points to ponder - for our personal growth through pain we actively experience:

Matthew Henry Commentary

*56:8-13 The heavy and continued trials through which many of the Lord's people have passed, **should teach us to be silent and patient under lighter crosses.***

*Yet we are **often tempted to repine and despond under small sorrows**. For this we should check ourselves.*

*David comforts himself, in his distress and fear, that God noticed all his grievances and all his grieves. **God has a bottle and a book for His people's tears, both the tears for their sins, and those for their afflictions**. He observes them with **tender concern**.*

*Every true believer may boldly say, The Lord is my helper, and then I will not fear what man shall do unto me; for **man has no power but what is given him from above**. Thy vows are upon me, O Lord; not as a burden, but as that by which I am known to be thy servant; as a **bridle that restrains me from what would be hurtful,** and directs me in the way of my duty.*

And vows of thankfulness properly accompany prayers for mercy. If God deliver us from sin, either from doing it, or by his pardoning mercy, he has delivered our souls from death, which is the wages of sin. Where the Lord has begun a good work, he will carry it on and perfect it.

David hopes that God would keep him even from the appearance of sin. ***We should aim in all our desires and expectations of deliverance, both from sin and trouble, that we may do the better service to the Lord; that we may serve him without fear.***

If his grace has delivered our souls from the death of sin, he will bring us to heaven, to walk before him for ever in light. (Psalm 56:8 Commentaries -Bible hub)

Ah, Hallelujah to that! May we be refreshed with a reframed mind-set, to see God in our walk of pain.

Inspiration

Letting go & letting God is not always our obvious choice when all seems bleak and grim in one's small world;

Yet, it remains the only plausible & sensible option for us to progress past survival mode...

As we rely on God's sufficient grace

He's faithful take us through raging storms;

At every point of need into exceeding victory.

Keep going for the gold, no matter what obstacles you encounter.

You're capable of rising above the challenges.

Let go of anxiety, and

Let God direct your path.

Immense peace,

As He walks you through it!

Prayer

Lord help us to learn to let go and

Allow you to transform our perspective to life. At times, simply...

Looking at creation, the great expanse of water in these oceans and seas

& the sky with an infinitely seamless end,

A flawless art & fusion of mere beauty!

Let us immerse ourselves in this indulgence

As it heightens the reality of and

Brings about such a sense of awe & calm,

A strong sense of serenity. a derivative to Your very creation, uniquely crafted for us.

May we learn to take a moment to breathe

In the stillness of this serene atmosphere.

Letting go of every negative vibe, while

Tapping in on all positive energies infused around us.

To be mindful of your flamboyant creation.

Teach us to dwell in peace, a place of rest

Immense peace...

May we know your extravagant love in this depiction of the beautiful creation, of us and of nature. Blended together into harmonious dependence on planet earth.

We give thanks and glory, to You.

Adaptation - TCASE. (02 Sept. '15)

Chapter 8

Shifting things in the heavenly places

Only because He is still fighting our battles though we may not physically see this.

"We are hard-pressed on every side, yet not crushed; we are perplexed, but not in despair; persecuted, but not forsaken; struck down, but not destroyed – "

God is in the business of shifting the atmosphere when we are in a state of brokenness. We may not always see this, but in those moments, is the call to give **God an offering of praise - in** depths of pain as a sacrifice. A heart of worship does reveal our strength in Him as He enables us. He accepts our offering.

It is inexplicable how the heart of worship has brought me to a place of sanity, immense peace and contentment in times that I felt desolate. Moments when I could not audibly utter a prescriptive prayer because I can neither focus on priority of needs nor eloquently articulate my needs to God. In such times, Jesus was praying for me...

"The Spirit you received does not make you slaves, so that you live in fear again; rather, the Spirit you received

brought about your adoption to sonship. And by him we cry, "Abba, Father."

The Spirit himself testifies with our spirit that we are God's children

Now if we are children, then we are heirs--heirs of God and co-heirs with Christ, if indeed we share in his sufferings in order that we may also share in his glory.

I consider that our present sufferings are not worth comparing with the glory that will be revealed in us. (Romans 8:15-18)

Then I would set myself at the feet of Jesus, gaze at him, hang about so I feel His presence, and just be.

No words, no communication, at times no action - just being present for Him to be accessible to me.

This eventually developed into moments of sweet fellowship as I 'communed' with him... in the silence. That sufficed for a season till it passed, and other times I'd be so dumbfounded and overwhelmed by problems so much that I knew all I needed was plead... again by visiting the foot of the cross.

I found myself often drifting into worship. The common and regular line for desperation was 'I surrender - here I am, down on my knees again'- as though God was prompting me, repeatedly, to surrender.

I would listen in to the words, sing from my heart of hearts and in no time at all, I'd find rest.

I was comforted as I praised, I was embraced as I sobbed, my tears were wiped as I cried out in despair -- and finally I would shift into a warm place of safety, a cuddle in the robe of righteousness. As Isaiah 61:10 states:

"I delight greatly in the LORD; my soul rejoices in my God. For he has clothed me with garments of salvation and arrayed me in a robe of his righteousness, as a bridegroom adorns his head like a priest, and as a bride adorns herself with her jewels."

I'd sense the Lord's cuddle, in a soft white cloak... the resurrection power overcoming all desperation. Soon I was energised and refilled sufficiently, to embark on the next battle after I have obtained mercy and been clothed in His grace:

"Therefore, since we have a great high priest who has ascended into heaven, Jesus the Son of God, let us hold firmly to the faith we profess.

For we do not have a high priest who is unable to feel sympathy for our weaknesses, but we have one who has been tempted in every way, just as we are – yet he did not sin.

Let us then approach God's throne of grace with confidence, so that we may receive mercy and find grace to help us in our time of need." (Hebrews 4:14-16 NIV)

What was happening, in those moments was the shifting of the atmosphere in the heavenly places - where sadness, was transformed into joy, pain was replaced by peace, fear was transformed into hope and my faith was ignited once again. I could see clearer after giving a praise-offering amidst my pain. I offloaded my cares, cast them onto the cross. Left them there till I could contend again.

Our actions, positive or negative... have the power to shift things in the spirit and effect them on earth. We should learn to profess good things. *And call those things that are not in existence as though they exist* (Romans 4:17)

Ministering Songs: I surrender & Steady in my heart-- Kari Jobe

One can cultivate and culture a habit of praising and worshipping God, in total surrender and stay steady in your faith.

Two songs have challenged me and oiled the hinges in my brokenness when I am in depths of indescribable pain.

Soak in His presence and meditate on the words, as if you own them and experience His glory. Let Him have his way in you.

I would implore you to have a listen to the splendid pieces by Hillsong. Except of lyrics:

'Here I am, **Down on my knees again,**

Surrendering all...

Find me here, Lord as You draw me near

Desperate for You...

Drench my soul, as mercy and grace unfold

I hunger and thirst... I surrender,

 I want to know You more

With arms stretched wide,

I know You hear my cry

Speak to me now, Speak to me now....

I surrender, I want to know You more-- (encore)

Lord have your way; Lord have your way... in me.

Inspiration

Positive Energy - dose on motivation, like a bath.

Enthusing oneself with positive energy is a must,

as a daily dose, even more important...

If you want to live a fulfilled life.

Everyday you're making a choice - be wise,

Get wisdom from God. -- TCASE. 16th July 2014

Shifting things in the heavenly places

Father God, our ABBA Father

We come before your throne of grace -- in Jesus Mighty name, during these... our troubled times.

I pray that you help me to focus on serving you.

Focus on doing the very best in every situation;

Being the best that I simply can be;

Making the most of and getting the best

Of every opportunity that presents itself.

Amidst all, to maintain an attitude of gratitude

With a positive mind-set at all times

To attract things from heavenly places --

As I shift my thinking into positivity

Despite the state of circumstances in my life.

Prayer

May God give us enough strength and

Sufficient grace to go through the refinery -

As we are purified into precious gold.

To find a sense of serenity,

Create a sanctuary around self…

To be content. For He makes all things new.

Peace, Be Still.

Chapter 9

When God is Silent

Intentionally Separated, to be set apart for God

The 'Buried Seed' germinates in such times, unwillingly or voluntarily - God waters the seed.

The past eight years or so were demanding on my life, on many fronts over varied significant issues requiring attention and God's involvement.

Without realising it, I had inevitably gone into a cocoon by imposition due to difficulties I faced. There was isolation following negative talk and misconceptions in some circles, that caused resentment and rejection in a subtle form. God was allowing things to unfold overtime. And things were revealed, slowly in different settings.

I worked hard to maintain sanity, but this meant kneeling at the feet of Jesus to be watered and refilled so that I could function. Over time I noticed that I shifted into a place of isolation. Here was separation from all the storms of life where God would plant a new seed in me, water it and I would germinate into a life-giving subject once again. As this had been depleted during the journey in the storm. Replenishment was not possible at the stage I was, I needed to be emptied, remoulded and refilled. This had to be in a place of separation.

He accomplished this by allowing, a temporal displacement into my life -- an illness crept in and it was to stay for a long time. In separation, God would allow NO unnecessary distractions, NO derailment. I had to be just in Him - 'while in the hallway of my pain. My discovery was that in the hallway is where God reveals Himself. I needed to keep my eyes fixated on Him and it was a rough ride. But His word encourages us to remain steadfast: "My heart, O God, is steadfast, my heart is steadfast; I will sing and make music."

The bigger the battle against forces of darkness, the louder and more diligent we must become in truth proclamation versus false accusations. To fix our gaze on Jesus and His Might, the ability of God's spirit to help us conquer in our battles. I learned this over time, learnt the hard way, that I was intentionally separated to be set apart.

Psalm 57:7 versions in KJV and NIV read:

"My heart is fixed, O God, my heart is fixed: I will sing and give praise."

"My heart, O God, is steadfast, my heart is steadfast; I will sing and make music."

Being aware of the depths of pain I was going through in the season; I was recently asked a 'million pound' question. One friend said, 'could I please open up and tell them what I need so that they could offer help wherever able'? My response is paraphrased in here.

It's operational support I desire, it includes 'human interaction' which I very much miss in recent years. I'm one who has always managed relationships. I can't tell you when I last had someone visit my house, just to say: 'how're you doing' - this is a quick stopover? Which I would always do with those I care for - being mindful of course that I can't impose myself on others if visits are unplanned. But stopping over sufficiently enough to 'oil hinges of the relationship' has always been priority on my task list, if I cannot have them come to my house or go out. I love people (so I believe) and enjoy spending time with them... One of the deepest expressions of love is the investment of time.

I continued to narrate - how I am always alone with children away, with my books or television - on gospel or you tube channels, in prayer, listening to messages or worship, writing, and doing mild chores I can afford to do, then going to work a few sessions midweek, back to routine -- picking up few voluntary work slots, and resting as needs be etc.

The cycle begins again...

No company, no surprise visits, no pleasant 'unexpected call' and I cannot just set off and go check on people (while I am managing a temporal illness - which needs respect as necessary).

I've been asking the Lord: what happened. When I was active, my house was always full... people flocking in and out, I frequently hosted, or someone would drop by, others pop-in when needing help or just a laugh.

Since I fell ill, all changed... it's gotten quieter and emptier in the home. In term time, it's my daughter in the temporary displaced state and myself in the temporarily disrupted situation. Lord, enlighten me. Previous day as I prayed in the morning, I asked again: Lord, do you see my loneliness, emptiness... the vacuum? Then After listening to/watching a few sessions of topics for the season, I sensed God saying - in these:

Moments of loneliness - commonly known to Him as *'aloneness'* rather than *loneliness* -- are when He is always with me; coupled with times of His silence; are when HE IS undoubtedly WITH ME. I could see the subject **When God is Silent** with clarity, in that moment as I tried to unpack the meaning of these words.

The emphasis became: these are the times when He is with me, around me and within me... so much that in fact, the... kind of 'tangible presence' that I seek in my cry... is not validated. In the still and quiet of my day... is where His presence is and I am missing it/ missing Him as I focus elsewhere.

It is in moments when He knows I've got everything that I have within me, around me while He's with me that He can be silent as I don't need other physical evidence. The Lord was suggesting that this 'alone time' offered the perfect recipe for satisfying my needs. Illustrated:

God's silence + man's absence = His affirmation of total presence and divine provision for the time.

The silence that I observed from my *displaced* desire (more tangible than the 'overhanging' presence I sensed); coupled with the absence of physical man, amounted to His way of affirmation. That all is well

- I lack nothing. Further revelation was that, the activities or company I desired in their form, would not allow me to look to Him to meet my needs. In that setting for my season, mankind would derail His desired focus from me to Him. This was wise counsel I'd never have considered. But it sparked my understanding of how God would separate Moses from everyone so that He could speak to him in the mountains. At times, He only allowed Aaron close - the *right calibre* of human presence for that season. All else would amount to distraction, and God spoke to Moses.

It became apparent that God was maturing me into knowing more of Him, whom I ever so consistently yearn to know more of... and HIS ways. As I insisted that I feel 'alone', there was more emphasis that He intentionally set me apart from the noise of this world, in order to enclose me, teach me more of Him and His ways. That the 'isolation' was not only a safer place, but also healthier place to be in -- in *this season*. I shared this as complete 'gibberish' - my thought-process and speak as I communed with God. And planned to shelve the information till the Lord would reveal His plan for accomplishing whatever the assignment of separation, isolation and seclusion.

Retrospectively, I realised that I did hear from God's prompting. This connection is a link that I treasure, having been established on the foundations of His love.

This friend had different ideas having been sensitive to the prompting of the Holy Spirit. I was propelled to get on board to encourage a soul or two with some detail we discussed. For those that desire to be enlightened and encouraged from this experience, through another broken vessel. I was to write all this out for sharing to impact lives... what? My learning - - separation, seclusion, isolation, 'aloneness' and any form of 'time out' from regular activities can be a time and place of rest, refreshing and for the setting-apart of God's children. He moulds them, equips them and empowers them to step out and go on 'assignment' - to accomplish His mission. He also reaffirms His presence as well as calm the child amidst the storms. I came out of there more placid, receptive and open-minded to the expanse of God's ability - we cannot contain Him.

I have learnt the art of submission, above all. To create a place of His rest, as -- a sanctuary for you and I is a place of His rest.

Inspiration

"Heaven is My throne,

And earth is My footstool.

Where is the house that you will build Me?

And where is the place of My rest? --- " Isaiah 66:1

The constant challenge in one's walk today...

To be a people that profess God's Supremacy,

Reflecting His power and influence in our lives.

To epitomise His very presence among us -

Let's strive to create a Sanctuary around us,

A place of His habitation, place of rest...

Emulating Christ through His love, embodied in us,

Lavishing others with kindness - for many desire it; I pray that our kindness lights up the world beyond us. One step. One day. One life at a time. In His Agape' love.

Prayer Points

"Behold, how good and how pleasant it is for brethren to dwell together in unity!" Psalm 133:1

May God Give us spiritual wisdom, to discern when we need to prepare a place of His rest, in separation.

May the Lord open opportunities and bring into our lives the right connections for every season - to propel us into His assignment.

Those with whom we can be intertwined and interlinked - - by and in His love.

Deeply routed by the completed work of the cross.

To activate the resurrection power as it encapsulates us all in a spirit of solidarity -- into a new dawn beyond current place of pain.

How good it is when brethren dwell in unity with the assurance that we are stronger together, in unity with each other and in our Creator.

Teach us Lord, to know and learn when we must go to a place of separation.

Amen.

Chapter 10

Harvest from the Refiner's Fire

'Alone Times are not Lonely Times' - what God breeds from the *'Alone Heart'* is to yield results (bear fruit) in total connectivity to the spirit.

Nobody wants to go through the refinery, but sometimes it is the purification process that moulds one's character into God's perfect will. His treasure, becomes the outcome of the gem He so intricately crafted us to be.

"He will sit as a refiner and a purifier of silver; He will purify the sons of Levi, and purge them as gold and silver, that they may offer to the Lord An offering in righteousness." - Malachi 3:3

"I will bring that group through the fire and make them pure. I will refine them like silver and purify them like gold. They will call on my name, and I will answer them. I will say, 'These are my people,' and they will say, 'The LORD is our God.'" - Zachariah 13:9

Perhaps your lonely place is where God is dealing with you to reconcile things to Himself, as He pleads your cause. *"For God was pleased to have all his fullness dwell in him, and through him to reconcile to himself all things, whether things on earth or things in heaven, by making peace through his blood, shed on the cross."* - Colossians 1:19-20 NIV

A crowd cannot always get on the ride with you to a place of special calling and purpose. Trust in His purpose – at times this is made perfect in a place where you have no choice but to listen in on His voice.

At times this is a separation of wheat from chaff.

"He is ready to separate the chaff from the wheat with his winnowing fork. Then he will clean up the threshing area, gathering the wheat into his barn but burning the chaff with never-ending fire." - Matthew 3:12

The purification process requires much submission and humility... allowing us to 'die to ourselves' by being broken, stripped of the old self and remoulded in alignment with His divine purpose of who He intended for us to be. His divine design to be revealed through us.

*"These have come so that the **proven genuineness of your faith--of greater worth than gold**, which perishes even though refined by fire--may result **in praise, glory and honour** when **Jesus Christ is revealed"**.* - 1 Peter 1:7 (NIV)

NLT version expands this as:

*"These trials will show that **your faith is genuine**. It is being **tested as fire tests and purifies gold** --though your faith is far more precious than mere gold. So when your faith remains strong through many trials, --it will **bring you much praise and glory and honour on the day when Jesus Christ is revealed to the whole world."***

At times this will require a sense of being short sold... we may get into betting with God - if this then I will. Or bargaining and negotiating for things we want our way. But the refiner empties us, strips off the old thinking in man and re-aligns that with a Godly and heaven-ward mind-set rather than an untoward... internal looking and self-seeking mind-set. This may happen over a time of resistance from us, but situations that we go through in life may at times inevitably gently shift our focus to the point of complete surrender - under duress.

At times, we may be overtaken by events - where God does not give us thinking time as there is too much freedom for the right decision to be made if one should 'think' through it. We realise that God has to take the wheel, we must let Him drive. Total surrender, imposed by life events.

He identifies the good traits in us and waters them as a seed, which germinates into the gem that He finally handpicked for His purposes to be delivered through. He expects us to present this gem, some form of a Christ-like prototype - to 'our' world in our everyday life, each and every encounter. That we conduct ourselves diligently with integrity and exude His grace. Consider rubbing this gem, the precious stone that has been refined, between your thumb and fingers and looking at the sparkle, crystallised effect to another' eye? This becomes God's view of the moulded you - which people see in you.

When we present this 'beauty' around our world, it begins to display and reflect God's harvest in us - His divine design... the crafted being who emulates their Maker. That replica of His very nature and image-- becomes His harvest.

It does not make us perfect in our own right, it makes us present *an imperfect and inadequate being, perfected by His love and qualified by His grace;* to act in His name as a joint heir to the throne of grace - adopted into sonship with Christ. Consider that, consider that truth and reality which we have at our disposal - by a mere acceptance of Christ, as our Lord and saving grace from all our ills. And it is a free gift to have

Him live in us so that He perfects us in His unfailing love.

Where you stand - with Him... is the poignant point to Him, if we have not aligned our thinking to know who He really is. He is a God of love, paying the full price on our behalf for ALL wrongs. We must wilfully graciously recognise this and say yes to Him. Say, yes - save me too, perfect me too, qualify me too. Then we will dwell with Him in His house forever.

Eternity is real... and so is hell. His mission preserves our lives to be in eternity with Him and all believing mankind and loved ones.

Inspiration: The Comfort Zone

The gem, holding it and rubbing it between one's fingers. Do you perceive its beauty?

Do you remain in the zone...? In or out?

Perhaps your lonely place is where God is dealing with you to reconcile things to Himself, as He pleads your cause.

A crowd cannot always get on the ride with you to a place of special calling and purpose.

Trust in His purpose – at times this is made perfect in a place where you have no choice but to listen in on His voice.

At times this is a separation of wheat from chaff

"He is ready to separate the chaff from the wheat with his winnowing fork. Then he will clean up the threshing area, gathering the wheat into his barn but burning the chaff with never-ending fire." Matt. 3:12

Find a sense of serenity, as you create a sanctuary around yourself... To be content. Peace, Be Still. (TCASE November 17, 2016)

Prayer

May God give us enough strength and

Sufficient grace to go through the refinery -

As we are purified into precious gold.

To find a sense of serenity,

Create a sanctuary around self...

To be content. For He makes all things new.

Peace, Be Still.

Chapter 11

A Receptive Attitude and Openness to Godly Things

Importance of obedience when He pursues you, in your place of pain. We know from scripture that obedience is far richer, better than sacrifice:

"But Samuel replied, what is more pleasing to the LORD: your burnt offerings and sacrifices or your obedience to his voice? Listen! Obedience is better than sacrifice, and submission is better than offering the fat of rams." (Samuel 15:22)

Do you sometimes feel as though you must pull up defences against people that you love and care for; and those that equally love and care for?

Do you find yourself protecting yourself, heart and emotions in situations! necessary for you to be yourself and feel at home? Do you find you must present a superficial front with certain, people or in certain situations because it's a more comfortable place for all parties - though realistically you're not being completely open?

These defences and protective mechanisms are derived from lack of safety and insecurities surrounding people or things and places in our lives. We 'adapt' our behaviours to fit the requirements of that scenario.

On the other hand, we may have other relationships where we can be... our other self and not feel the need to put up an act, out on a show or fit in the designated box. Because we are in a place of safety and liberation. We can say and do anything with no fear of repercussions. There are no major consequential effects arising from the performance or lack of... any actions in the company or location in these scenarios. It is an intimate relationship that God desires with His children – and it is in those moments that He reveals to them the hidden thing that they would never know.

That -- is the kind of relationship God wants to develop and nurture in us. He is excited to know we can be ourselves with Him. In any case, we know that 'Nothing in all creation is hidden from God's sight. Everything is uncovered and lay bare before the eyes of Him to whom we must give account.'

With that in mind, we might as well culture a habit of honesty and openness with God. He knows all things before they happen, they're part of His creation of heaven and earth, and the formation of its hosts... when we open up and allow selves to get close to God, He acknowledges this and draws close to us. Scripture says, *'draw nigh unto me and I will draw nigh unto you'*... this means we pursue Him and He in return pursues us - for a deeper and meaningful relationship.

"By the word of the Lord the heavens were made,

And all the host of them by the breath of His mouth. Let all the earth fear the Lord;

Let all the inhabitants of the world stand in awe of Him. For He spoke and it was done; He commanded, and it stood." Psalm 33:6/8-9

"Short as life is, we make it still shorter by the careless waste of time." - Victor Hugo.

Today, transform every negative thought, and experience into a stepping stone to the next stage and level of accomplishment...

Transparency is key.

Aiming with all determination to overcome fear and a sense of condemnation, because we are forgiven in Christ and awarded freedom...

As we know from God's word: *where the Spirit of the Lord is... there is freedom.*

"Casting down arguments and every high thing that exalts itself against the knowledge of God, bringing every thought into captivity to the obedience of Christ," – 2 Corinthians 10:5--

Life is a journey, complete it!

In my experience about this journey, I have a friend who always made me believe in myself, through our communication lines. She has often alluded that I write, speak, talk poetic... weirdest things I would say.

I was offered an opportunity to contribute on a platform that will encourage others. To write about my journey... as coming from my heart due to some information I would share about my burdens in this life. My transparent life would be of value and worth of sharing. Unbeknownst to me, they were in network connection that would support on a platform to share my life experience.

Once I was asked, realised I was reminded to rekindle the dying fire within, igniting the passion to share via snippets I'd intended to entitle in words to encapsulate the message: 'Trusting God in The Hallway - and Praising God While In the storm'.

Victory - Storm = a waiting period»» active pain

I sensed God prompting for a release of a series on Ministering from a place of pain; while in active pain.

Taking His lead and hopefully deliver within this year - for access to those in high storms as an encouragement resource.

To equip the broken hearted with coping strategies by opening the road into my heart for others to read my experiences. That would mean for a moment stepping into anxiety in terms of how comfortable this deep level of connecting with the external world will be. This would be invading my place of peace and position me into vulnerability!

Peace: did I really have it by keeping all this in, or do l cultivate it by giving other people. In which case that will bring about real peace. Well I had never thought of this...

I thought of my present world as it sits, wondered how the story or two I'd share would be perceived. How I'd be analysed... but the spirit reminded me - Again on the journey I've embarked on in recent years - to allow judgments to fall off and drop off anything negative that would pre-empt my delivery.

Scripture reminds us in Hebrews 4:12-13:

Let us therefore be diligent to enter that rest, lest anyone fall according to the same example of disobedience.

For the word of God is living and powerful, and sharper than any two-edged sword, piercing even to the division of soul and spirit, and of joints and marrow, and is a discerner of the thoughts and intents of the heart.

And there is no creature hidden from His sight, but all things are naked and open to the eyes of Him to whom we must give account.

Chapter 12

Your Designed Destiny

When God orders your steps, the 'envisioned' illusions, dreams and mere thoughts amount to true visions, spirit led dreams and spiritual revelations:

"And afterward, I will pour out my Spirit on all people. Your sons and daughters will prophesy, your old men will dream dreams, your young men will see visions." Joel 2:28

Early confirmation in dreams or a simple 'picture in my mind' proved that I could foresee things.

In early years of marriage, we had numerous car accidents, I would only comprehend in retrospect due to detail of the accident - which turned out to be the reality - as on many occasions happenstances mirrored similar setting to what I'd seen in my dreams.

Prior dreams to significant events followed a timeline:

In 2002, having a strong sense over my oldest sister who'd been taken quite ill on one asthma episode, I requested that she be shifted to my family home to enable parents care for her. I recall sharing this information with siblings in a somewhat commanding voice over telephone call - that if this was not done we may have far-reaching consequences. It was within a few months after this that my big sister Evelyn took God's call aged 49.

Prior to this I had lost two big brothers - Frank at 43 in 1998, after nursing prolonged illness; and Mike at 41 after an accident in his home in 2000. The former was a development I somewhat prepared for - as I had gone home to visit brother while in hospital on one occasion, and again to 'bid farewell' when it became apparent his days were numbered -- few weeks prior. The latter event was a shock to family... but God saw us through.

Then, a vivid recollection of me in attendance of brother Tony, 'at his funeral'. I recall how I cried painfully in the dream. I understood what God was preparing me for, when within a couple years Anthony Victor answered God's call in 2004 aged 39.

From 2009-10 onwards I had one child as a student living away from home studying. I oft found out about **worsening** illness (which included frequent fainting episodes) in an intuition that something was wrong during intervals of these incidents. Until I confronted her, she would create some distance in those times. She would reveal information only when I would call - in confession that she withheld this to 'protect me'.

These experiences have intensified in recent years - included 'thoughts' I processed regarding Victoria in 2011 on one evening as I prepped for church service. The thoughts I processed at that point and immediate attempt to call her after church - revealed the reality that she had been in hospital for a few hours that day, and took God's call within minutes of my failed attempted call to her on 9th January 2011 - aged 46.

Over Christmas season, the birth of the Messiah has always been a reminder of the reinforcement of the Old Testament as He brings the new covenant.

Most recent experiences - how God has evidently spoken again during past Christmas and in new year, and confirmed almost every **significant** word (own descriptions of a situation, scripture I've thought of and Bite-sized/mini 'devotions-to-self' I've written). So significant that I have spoken in my mind, in word and through prayer or via encouragement to someone in need, in inspirational messages I have written - they have been confirmed and/or backed up by the Holy Spirit through a sermon, in a counselling session or in daily devotional and other Scriptural readings in the day/period immediately after.

"'In the last days, God says, I will pour out my Spirit on all people. Your sons and daughters will prophesy, your young men will see visions, your old men will dream dreams. "Acts 2:17

This has affirmed what I considered as my intuitive thinking -- as being not directly from my soul, but a prompting by the Holy Spirit. This experience intensified in January 17, most frequently in each day, to the extent I have begun to think some experiences seem like I am placed in a continual state of *deja vu.* Thus, confirmation that God continues in His intent to engage us and a trigger for me to tune in intently.

To be intentional about stopping and making the time to hear Him, creating an atmosphere where He knows I am waiting with anticipation. This mirrors the teaching and emphasis in other chapters on creating a solitary place... this can also be on the go - creating space in your mind for solitude - holding all forward thoughts and judgment and make room for Him to be at a place of rest... around you.

I am still learning to discipline myself to be habitual in commitment. Seclude yourself, mentally and emotionally for His Spirit to inhabit your inner being. During normal daily living activities, this approach works too.

Develop the habit and in time, your mind will be retrained to operate in that mode, in autopilot. This grows faith into greater heights.

Refiner's Fire purifies through storms and affirms who we are, created in His image... Divine design.

He is a God of order and can work through things in a structured manner to systematically channel you to the **Designed Destiny**; ordering steps to go into places, by mere thought, strategic order or at times propelling you there, without giving you any 'thinking time' -' as that window may make you over-think actions and possibly derail you.

At times, He will work in a chaotic situation, and move you to a specific place... only to discover God spoke (Joseph, the dreamer).

One depiction of a future happenstance took place in 2013.

Two pictures of an eagle - each one of the strongest, most powerful and intellectually wisest bird. Second picture depicted the Eagle on a tree, which was basically all dry with only one piece protruding out...

branched off upwards to the side. It formed a V-shape... and on this was the Eagle which seemed trapped by its resting place-- the branch.

It had already caught its prey in the sea/ocean beneath it... yet was unable to retrieve or redeem itself from this spot to rise above its obstacle and fly 'fly above the storm' into safety as it's known to do so well.

TRAPPED - NO WAY OUT, Prey in hand... seemingly comfortable in its normal place of rest.

Why two eagles on separate pictures that 'spoke to me? A depiction of strength?

This took place in 2013, as I attended one residential course on a programme I was pursuing, the facilitator asked us to pick any one (or two) out of approximately 200 images... an image that would seem appealing to us / we would be attracted to. We then had to explain to our action group sets. Why the pictures and interpret any hidden meanings. I knew instantly what the images represented, which I narrated... though I still doubted internally. To my 'shock' what I saw then was a preparation to a situation that I would experience two years later - but as I had seen it in spirit, God had psychologically prepared me so that I'd then go through this storm (trap) with His grace despite difficulties I encountered each day for nearly an eighteen-month period.

This has been one of most recent affirmations that God speaks in subtle ways. Yet we oft miss His voice... it is a subtle, 'still small voice'. It took two years for the situation to unfold, but God spoke to me in advance so I was psychologically and spiritually prepared... and took a step of faith to continue to trust Him. Between mid-year 2013 and mid-year 2015, I had lost a stable job, triggered by a recently crept in illness, which in fact transpired to be 'medically' diagnosed as a chronic illness with functionality difficulties. As I speak, I still contend with a role in what I call *'Alternating self-management and caring package' for one daughter - in a temporarily displaced state and myself in the temporarily disrupted situation.*

As we have **'Temporary'** on going 'medically diagnosed' illnesses. I call 'medically' because I believe ABBA Father's power to transform those reports into something positive... a good report and refute that of a grasshopper mentality...

All I now know is that God is still working in me, polishing me, sharpening my skills and enhancing my abilities to stand tall, holding my head high and chinning me up -- so His divine plan is accomplished through me and unleash the designed destiny into existence. I am not there yet... but I am in position to receive what has already been agreed and set out for me in the heavenly places, as my destiny. I am positioned to receive that and then deliver that from the fullness of my bosom... which I am now certain God is continually watering -- in this season. The seed germinates in growth and maturity for harvest, this feels like a painful process in the here and now. Yet when harvest comes, the seed will have borne much fruit to feed all the hungry within those compounds and boundaries - perhaps even, beyond the surrounding borders. That's where I'm positioned to be - the prophesied Joseph was to feed a nation. I, too... will.

The Razor Blade Analogy and God's Approach

A wise poet once said, 'A razor blade was never sharpened by velvet' {excerpt - Mills, S-M & Smit, N: From the heart, with applications, (1995)}.

This provides content in the knowledge and truth that a blade is only as effective as it's sharpened state enables it to function. Once blunt, it's functionality is lost and is pretty much rendered 'useless'. Only two options arise from this state - the Owner is justified to:

o Rightfully **discard** the dysfunctional razor blade with the intent of replacing it

o Preferably **sharpen** the dysfunctional, *blunt and used* razor blade with the intent of restoring it back to its functional state.

What God refrains from is exercising the right to discard the dysfunctional tool -- is He able to replace a complete replica with the exact same specifications to accomplish His plan. The destiny He originally designed meets the spec for the first tool, not its replica or prototype. So, He doesn't quite pick this option as feasible for the designed destiny to be reached with His plans duly accomplished. He wants the same vessel with original traits and character to deliver His purposes.

The optimum solution becomes the sharpening of this very dysfunctional tool which He holds as He still has use for to deliver His designed destiny for that tool - set apart as a vessel for accomplishment of His purposes in life. While God works at restoring the tool to its former glory, there will be the inevitable resistance arising from the contending enemy who wants to topple God's plans. Similarly, we as the vessel resist this process as we find the sharpening too unbearable to carry through on this journey. The walk suddenly becomes painful -- We ask God - why? Why are you asleep on the boat?

I posit before you - this razor blade analogy.

Are you now in a place to fathom God's love and His actions... even as He takes us through a storm, so He can bring us out of it transformed for a plan? This is a refining process, it's uncomfortable, and it's painful. It's 'lonely', it's rough and tough... as a journey. But it's for His purpose, His glory.

Dare to trust, that the product will be purified gold, precious... just the gem God intended to be - for your designed destiny.

Inspiration

Your Designed Destiny is within your reach

Go for the gold, dream big & take the necessary steps towards your goal post.

The journey through preparation for the future is never smooth, but rough and tough as in training ground for a marathon for an athlete or a soldier for the battle field.

Put on own your gear to run the marathon, qualified to do while in training;

And the fighting armour - for the battle field - qualified only in training.

Carry your instructions in your mind for instant mental retrieval at each point of need.

Equally, equip your soul for a spiritual battle. Ability to mentally retrieve your instructions

Relies on the mental capacity following training...

Put on therefore, the whole armour of God

So that you may stand firm against the fiery darts.

You have that dream in mind because God laid it in you, for your Designed Destiny

He gives you spiritual potential in His word

You have the physical potential to deliver it.

Partner with God and dis-align with the enemy

To reach your goal in fulfilment of

God's plan for you.

He has a distinctive design for your destiny

Walk there, find it - accept it. Live it.

-- TCASE 10th July 2014 (adapted)

Chapter 13

Unleashing Infinite Freedom

There is freedom - even in midst of pain. God has taught me this in the season He is walking me through at present.

"Now the Lord is the Spirit, and where the Spirit of the Lord is, there is freedom.

And we all, who with unveiled faces contemplate the Lord's glory, are being transformed into his image with ever-increasing glory, which comes from the Lord, who is the Spirit." 2 Corinthians 3:17-18

Freedom covers many areas which arise from conduct commonly perceived as normal behaviour. Because nobody ever stops to think about it - how they carry themselves or behave. In a world where the norm is viewed as self-defeating proclamations for instance - freedom must prevail. Behaviour arising from our subconscious minds may include any form of negativity towards self or others. May arise from inner self via self-degradation; low self-esteem and lack of confidence. Or externally through rejection, negative demeanour, belittling attitude from others.

Yet we know God reminds us that where His spirit is, there also is freedom. That freedom reigns and gives His promise as a prophesy for every trial - He will give you a way of escape:

"No temptation has overtaken you except such as is common to man; but God is faithful, who will not allow you to be tempted beyond what you are able, but with the temptation will also make the way of escape, that you may be able to bear it." 1 Corinthians 10:13.

I once prayed two 'simple' prayers -- without comprehension of the extent to deeper meanings in practical terms - inspired by Hillsong worship 'Hosanna' and 'Oceans - where Feet may fail'

"Heal my heart and make it clean

Open up my eyes to the things unseen

Show me how to love like You have loved me

Break my heart for what breaks Yours

Everything I am for Your Kingdom's cause

As I walk from earth into eternity" and

"Spirit lead me where my faith is without borders-

Let me walk upon the waters - wherever you'd call me…

Take me deeper than my feet would ever wander

Where my faith would be made stronger

In the presence of my saviour..."

Thus, I was committing myself to any extents of service that God deemed necessary for me to undertake, with no confinement to familiar zones but beyond my expectations

And break my heart for what breaks His?

I saw very painful things thrown in my way... at times battles required fasting to remain in focus and crying out... Lord I don't know how to do this.... the last 6 months were indescribably challenging. But God has fought battles, winning one at a time.

This is now week 8 into 2017 and God has been revealing a few things to me. He has intimated that it is a period of new beginnings - the number 8 represents that in biblical terms. I must believe Him and just walk, follow as He guides - to a place of victory as we begin anew, afresh, refreshed vision, refreshed anointing.

Today is Tuesday 21st February 2017. I am laying on my comfy couch in my living room... tuned in to -

listen intently and intentionally to God. I'm unwell but giving thanks that I am comfortable. I'm not going to worry about or feel sorry for 'me'.

As I write this book, for the whole period I have been 'couch bound'. I have been too unwell to go to work and too weak to do basic chores and normal personal tasks - I simply cannot follow any routine without the risk of being completely incapacitated in the aftermath.

I mention in other chapters that I manage a temporal illness. It is medically diagnosed as CFS/ME (Chronic Fatigue Syndrome/ Myalgic Encephalomyelitis) - simplified as debilitating and complex disorder characterised by intense fatigue that is not improved by bed rest and that may be worsened by physical or mental activity. Usually triggered by viral infection, tragedy, trauma, bereavement and such tough life experiences.

At week six into my illness. The doctor suggested after I'd attempted resuming work on the previous Thursday: "Let's try booking you off one more week and then I must review you..."

I said okay. Times have changed, I now know the benefits of being on rest when unwell. I would ordinarily fight that proposal... but I have freedom to know that when the body needs rest, I must allow it. Before, I'd argue and say that the world needs me to do XYZ. It would imply that the world (my world) - will stop if I don't get up and go.... how funny! And indeed, hilarious in God's eyes, somewhat. Because He has the ultimate control and the world cannot stop as long as He is in control and on the throne - until eternity.

I'd think that being at home for bed rest due to the illness will pull me down further. This used to be my perspective when I first fell ill four years ago, and officially took time off work – albeit under duress. Taking time off was practically imposed by combination of three human interventions.

My daughters insisted that I needed a doctor's assessment when I thought I was in control but they saw a different, deteriorating Mum in her abilities. When I became short of speech one evening, unable to converse, and slurred speech being prominent, they took it upon themselves to book me a doctor's appointment - and just instructed me to be there the following morning.

A week later, my Manager insisted that I needed medical input as I didn't look my normal self. Eventually my doctor emphasised that I needed to slow down and nurture me (not everyone else, for a change, after a couple of weekly reviews - while they worked through uncovering what the illness entailed. There was no indication of possible diagnosis for a very long time. A possible brain tumour, stroke, neurosis and related conditions... were all on the table for elimination.

I had to quickly learn to slow down, be at peace and allow my body to respond to necessary repair. This meant being at peace with my rebellious body, which seemed to have 'attacked' me. I had to work harmoniously with it to help me function. That journey begun by April-May 2013.

Don't feel sorry for yourself...

Since then, I have thanked God for the illness which has still enabled to do certain things. I began to look for all positive things within the limitations I had. I praised God and thanked Him that I was even able to say prayers and worship Him. This included negotiations with Him on how far this situation would go... became I wasn't ready to be 'trapped' and lose the normalcy that I was familiar to. But this was a long big lesson. 'it doesn't happen to others... it happens to you too.

You are now 'that woman with a 'long-term medical condition' -- but still knows her Maker is in the infirmity with her'.

You're now 'the lady who cares for her daughter with a chronic illness but also has an ongoing illness herself ' -- but she praises her God through it.

'You are now the lady who does not lose heart over all this... because her Redeemer lives'.

How long? This was to be determined by what God's next plan for my life was. I had to come to terms and be at peace with this reality... so out of my control and entrusting it into His control. I found immense peace, a release from a burden and utter freedom.

Within the infirmity, and the added responsibility to keep supporting one daughter with daily functioning. He was there, peaks and troughs were imminent - but He was there.

I had to stop positioning myself in a place of sorrow and sadness, into a place of liberation and freedom. At times, I have observed people who learn of my struggles feeling sorry for me. Yet, I have been taken on a journey not to – it's not acceptance or succumbing to the situation, rather a shifted mindset, so that worry does not conquer me. It took God walking me through that view of myself into freedom. I accept emphatic gestures - but as I get to know people more, I do present that image of God.

God doesn't want me to feel sorry for myself, He has given me freedom. Freedom and peace even in infirmity- as Job intimated - I knew my Redeemer lives. In the process, I've been consistently reminded by God that I am intentionally separated to be set apart.

Joey's walk and nuggets of wisdom

My big girl Jo said to me a few days ago, that she had come to terms with the new person she now is. Suggesting that she had thought through and meditated on her current state of events. realised that she lost the past five-six years of her life, in terms of who she was and wanted to be, who she knew and believed herself to be. Alluding that in acceptance of the loss, she experienced a light bulb moment as she discovered that she had been mourning the loss of herself, the person that she was. Her aspirations and the journey she planned to follow had proved unfruitful due to the illness she suffers from.

That was a different phase of her life. To move forward she needed to 'give herself permission to mourn herself'; and thereafter accept and embrace her new reality. That it's ok not to know where she was going next if God knows. Finally embrace this fact and assume the role of the individual that God created her to be.

This struck a chord on me... I was touched, humbled and challenged. I realised that I too, perhaps need to mourn her loss and embrace the re-packaged Jo that God has wrapped up with a specific plan for her life. To hand over to God, while I remain on standby and accessible if she needs me. But only, 'on call' for her. This was a release of freedom, unleashed in shifting a perspective as God guided through her in that time. I was challenged, but it was evident that freedom has been unleashed, more so in handing over to God – which was total proof of the work of the spirit. This was on a Friday afternoon, as we sat in the car having returned from a second hospital appointment with her – she needed treatment. We were to wait through the weekend to assess how she would cope following a mini procedure which was indicating potential complexity.

The Joey Confidence and Trust Analogy

Following a mini op my daughter had, we experienced minor challenges – including a massive swelling in her face. Two mornings after this event, she dropped into my room before I arose. Kneeling by my side she softly asked a simple question as she pointed at her cheek 'is this going down?'

'Yes,' I said. She held my hand, said a short prayer... and off she went.

Confident that I gave her a true answer. That's it - she's content, she has freedom off this worry.

A nudge from God as I thought... 'wow, how trusting and truly dependent children are on us - it is so amazing'.

Then... smiling internally, I thought jokingly: 'as though it were God and the child'.

Which, in fact God was presenting to me. That's precisely how He is with me, why can't I equally trust Him?

God was asking me: 'Why can't you just trust my simple answer to you, when I say things in the same way you said to Jo: "it's going to be ok"? She was content and confident - it was okay.

Yet you want to see fire come down to believe what I say. But, I work in simple familiar terms all the time, to not overwhelm you. Drop the worry, trust and go to play!'

I have taken this on board - when God says it, that settles it! Abba Father has said it is okay many times. How often do we believe? That's our lesson.

The Joey Confidence & Trust Analogy and nuggets of wisdom have been further proof that during challenges in life, one can still walk in freedom. These are most recent events which have reinforced the need to hold God's perspective of the situations that we contend with. In Him we feel safe, contrary to what the enemy would intend. Hallelujah to the Lamb of God.

We ought to acknowledge, it takes the spirit of God to defy all odds of infirmity, brokenness, desolation and distress into freedom, into Jubilee as Jesus proclaims all the good things.

That dis-arms the enemy as we align and partner with God's will. Thus, our challenge is to defy all odds and go against what the enemy places before our eyes-- that we see a mountain but proclaim a breakthrough, without being moved. Because God does not give us a spirit of fear...

"For God did not give us a spirit of timidity or cowardice or fear, but [He has given us a spirit] of power and of love and of sound judgment and personal discipline [abilities that result in a calm, well-balanced mind and self-control]." 2 Timothy 1:7 AMP

And we know we can only achieve this spiritual perspective by being empowered in spirit, by God's grace. Where the spirit of the Lord is... is Infinite freedom, not for a moment, for a purpose - pure Infinite Freedom -- in spite of the storms.

Confined to a couch but thankful to God as He speaks to me. Thankful that though I'm exhausted and feel 'awful' - I still have reasonable cognitive abilities today - to be able to share this with you.

I believe God is not finished with His intentional separation - 'to set me apart' - for such a season as this. He releases me into Infinite Freedom.

May His glory be revealed, in my brokenness. In my infirmity - our infirmities - my daughter and I; and any of you that still await restoration.

His glory is what our hearts long for.

Inspiration

God gives man the freedom of choice, and guidance through His word in distinguishing between good & bad.

Let's make the right choices and reject the wrong, under His guidance.

Have a productive week!

-- TCASE - 30th June 2014.

Chapter 14

Divine Sustenance into Designed Destiny

God reminds us that He will adequately resource us in the moments of need because He is with us and will NEVER forsake but remains around us.

We Need the sustenance of God's grace in the wilderness that lies between our calling and the Promised Land - as Sue Gorst alludes.

"And God is able to make all grace abound to you, so that having all sufficiency in all things at all times, you may abound in every good work." - 2 Corinthians 9:8 (ESV)

Though His grace is sufficient, we do recognise that Paul remained with a thorn in his flesh. He pleaded with God to remove that thorn, but God's perspective was different.

At times the afflictions we go through are allowed by God for the perfecting of our faith. Is our faith seasonal, reliant on our circumstances or it is real -- in the valley of death and in the highways, we profess our faith?

We must **be steadfast in our faith and walk with God, so that His** grace abounds in an outpouring and continual flow from the fountain of God's love.

Into the restoration walk, lest we falter or our faith wavers.

Moses was ushered into a mission to take the Israelites to the Promised Land and said that 'my presence will not go with you' - because the Israelites had been obstinate and stiff-necked in their conduct before God (Exodus 32:9-10)

."And the Lord said to Moses, "I have seen this people, and indeed it is a stiff-necked people! Now therefore, let Me alone, that My wrath may burn hot against them and I may consume them. And I will make of you a great nation..." (NKJV)

However, Moses had the nerve to ask God and plead with Him once again... 'if your presence does not go with us then don't send me there ... how with the people of the face of earth know that these are your people.

In effect Moses was challenging God to Redeem Himself, to Redeem His reputation as a true God, a good Father and that He had capacity to melt His anger even though it had 'waxed hot' against His children.

We see in this story how an intercessor's prayer can change God's actions... God softened His heart and forgave His people.

God said because you have asked, my presence will go with you and you shall find favour (grace) in my sight.

Then Moses said to God, "See, You say to me, 'Bring up this people.' But You have not let me know whom You will send with me.

Yet You have said, 'I know you by name, and you have also found grace in My sight.' Now therefore, I pray, if I have found grace in Your sight, show me now Your way, that I may know You and that I may find grace in Your sight. And consider that this nation is Your people."

And He said, "My Presence will go with you, and I will give you rest." Then he said to Him, "If Your Presence does not go with us, do not bring us up from here. For how then will it be known that Your people and I have found grace in Your sight, except You go with us? So we shall be separate, Your people and I, from all the people who are upon the face of the earth."

So the Lord said to Moses, "I will also do this thing that you have spoken; for you have found grace in My sight, and I know you by name." And he said, "Please, show me Your glory." Then He said, "I will make all My goodness pass before you, and I will proclaim the name of the Lord before you. I will be gracious to whom I will be gracious, and I will have compassion on whom I will have compassion." But He said, "You cannot see My face; for no man shall see Me, and live." And the Lord said, "Here is a place by Me, and you shall stand on the rock. So it shall be, while My glory passes by, that I will put you in the cleft of the rock, and will cover you with My hand while I pass by. Then I will take away My hand, and you shall see My back; but My face shall not be seen." Exodus 33:12-23 NKJV

Moving forward as you march towards your destiny, remember that God is with you. But in His assurance, He also asks that we should be strong and courageous, in the knowledge of His presence surrounding us.

"Have I not commanded you? Be strong and of good courage; do not be afraid, nor be dismayed, for the Lord your God is with you wherever you go."

'Do not depart from the book of this law but meditate on it day & night' Joshua 1:4-9

"Be strong and of good courage, do not fear nor be afraid of them; for the Lord your God, He is the One who goes with you. He will not leave you nor forsake you" - Deuteronomy 31:6

"Wait on the Lord; Be of good courage, And He shall strengthen your heart; Wait, I say, on the Lord!" - Psalm 27:14

Losses and His Divine Sustainable Provisions

I have narrated some events relating to my losses. These comprise bereavement, health, financial freedom and stability, career/job, and consequential impact on self-worth as derivative to my challenges -- these have all largely been triggered by the loss of my health.

I have learnt and been challenged in these times, to rely on God's supernatural and divine providence. He is the source in fulfilment of needs. While this is not always physically evident, it is evident in all other aspects of my being as I live. I have a deep peace about me even when I cannot see where from, when and how my next provision will 'comfortably' emerge. I have such strong faith and a sense of freedom about these uncertainties to a point that it sometimes 'scares' me -' that I am unworried about it... such faith that I hold my peace as I know God fights my battles.

"Therefore I say to you, do not worry about your life, what you will eat or what you will drink; nor about your body, what you will put on. Is not life more than food and the body more than clothing?" Mathew 6:25

At times, we cannot see anything positive enough to thank God for. But we need to be simplistic and look at the basic needs of life. But consider this...

The very reason you're able to 'complain' is because you have received a special gift today... your very life!

Will you take the challenge then?

Thank God for the mere gift of life-- this is enough. That you've breath and are healthy and strong is enough reason to thank God - be intentional about seeing God's blessings, counting them one by one. You will be surprised at how much God has blessed you. In the midst of difficulties, there is still reason to praise.

Additionally, looking around us and being mindful of the brightness and positive things surrounding us means we are more drawn to holding an attitude of gratitude.

Appreciating and admiring creation, the great expanse of water and the sky, with an infinitely seamless end is a flawless art and fusion of beauty that God has presented us. Enjoy it...

The recognition of simple things, good and wonderful things heightens the reality of contentment in our lives. It brings about such a sense of calm, a sense of serenity.

Take a moment to breathe in the stillness of this serene atmosphere,

Letting go every negative vibe while tapping in onto all positive energy released around and infused into you.

You will be surprised at the amount of grace you will experience abounding, and a release of simply, Immense peace!

Inspiration - For our warfare is not carnal

Do you feel disheartened, and at times wonder where the next 'device of the enemy' might just come from?

Be bold, you hold stronger and most effective strategies. Your Protector - Jehovah EL SHADDAI is mightier than the uncertain circumstances before you.

Partner with Him as He equips you to conquer those forces.

***Your duty:** position yourself into a place of victory by claiming and receiving His promises.*

You MUST ACT in agreement with God to 'dis-align' & disengage yourself from the evil forces.

For our warfare is non-carnal:

"--but mighty in God for pulling down strongholds,

--- Casting down arguments and every high thing that exalts itself against the knowledge of God,

---bringing every thought into captivity to the obedience of Christ," - excerpt: 2 Corinthians 10

Last year, my husband and I celebrated our silver wedding anniversary.

It was one more reality that brought home God's faithfulness -- how He was us through to this point was yet another miracle. I intimated this in recognising that to everything there is a time - now is the time to give honour to God.

The Mastermind & Sovereign Power who relentlessly 'Guided, Governed and Guarded' our matrimonial union for 25 years - in a world and culture where quitting is probably largely perceived as becoming the norm and even so more of an attractive option than sticking through it. We both had times when we assessed why people would 'throw in the towel'. But God would reveal to each the value that we have in each other. A deep love that keeps us bound enough to yearn for better and find a way out of situations. God kept us going and has made us stronger over the years. And that's how God works with us – patiently, on second chances.

So, it became more apparent that I had multitudes of reasons to bless the Lord... simply because I knew my story. We survived in a setting of a story of two imperfect parties, who were governed by a Perfect Father... Over years in training, disciplining and correction, ridicule of the Holy Spirit and His grace led us to one place. By ultimately comprehending that the only winning strategy was to look up to the

RIGHT source for direction on running the institution - institution of marriage. And not resource ourselves, with failing strategies.

Over the years, I have recognised that mastering my own crafted plan ought to give - so that God's perfect plan prevails. I have learnt to only look to Him as the constant guide. Or else there are dire consequences.

This was another victory - won through sustenance by God's grace. Divine sustenance into a place of victory, into God's designed destiny for my life. Hallelujah because He lives.

Simple Prayer

May God open our spiritual eyes

So we can perceive the world around us

From 'His Lenses, His perspective and His perfect view' of who we are;

In the bigger picture of our lives in its entirety.

And embrace each other as He embraces us - with deep affection and the unconditional love He displays.

Agape'!

Chapter 15

Recognising Him as Your Rear Guard

There are sometimes conditions we must meet and observe. When **perseverance yields a harvest.**

At times results from the Refiner's fire are displayed in traits and character we see in other people. Sometimes the perseverance through hardships breeds a resistance to succumbing to challenging circumstances.

Some of us have learnt that obedience to God's instructions bears much. For others, it is training ground which brings them to a point of realisation.

"Is this not the fast that I have chosen: To loose the bonds of wickedness,

To undo the heavy burdens,

To let the oppressed go free,

And that you break every yoke?

Is it not to share your bread with the hungry,

And that you bring to your house the poor who are cast out;

When you see the naked, that you cover him,

And not hide yourself from your own flesh?

--Then your light shall break forth like the morning,

Your healing shall spring forth speedily,!

And your righteousness shall go before you;

The glory of the Lord shall be your rear guard.

Then you shall call, and the Lord will answer;

You shall cry, and He will say, 'Here I am.'

"If you take away the yoke from your midst,

The pointing of the finger, and speaking wickedness,

If you extend your soul to the hungry

And satisfy the afflicted soul,

---Then your light shall dawn in the darkness,

And your darkness shall be as the noonday.

The Lord will guide you continually,

And satisfy your soul in drought,

And strengthen your bones;

You shall be like a watered garden,

And like a spring of water,

---

whose waters do not fail.

Those from among you

Shall build the old waste places;

You shall raise up the foundations of many generations;

And you shall be called the Repairer of the Breach,

The Restorer of Streets to Dwell In." Isaiah 58

He becomes the Jehovah Jireh, blessing us in divine providence...

"He gathers the waters of the sea together as a heap; He lays up the deep in storehouses." Psalm 33:7

You may find people sharing life stories which blow the mind in how God walked them out of difficult places. At times the experiences have had *'obedience as a condition for restoration'* and another's wholly dependent on God's grace. The restored have accepted Jehovah Jireh as their provider, their Rear Guard in times of need, in and out of season.

They share testaments of restoration - past the depths of storms. Through refining they appear to be gifted and skilled in articulation of their journey. We admire them, we honour them, and we commend them.

Quite oft these individuals do not even realise that they are as 'powerful and eloquent' as we perceive them to be. Because the 'getting there' was never a smooth ride for them... but we only see the flamboyance.

Yet, there's A Significant Storyline behind the Flamboyance!

Perhaps this resonates – when and in what conditions would you wish for the flamboyance –In spite of its preparatory process– or would you rather not...?

At times, we hear someone speak, offer an inviting gesture or utter a soft word — provide direction or encouragement — even rendering a service through such a comforting touch that overwhelms us. They are articulate and eloquent. Simple.

We are amazed at how gracious and well-spoken the individual happens to be. Or indeed how blessed and gifted they are... instantly, thoughts may be: 'how I wish I could be that 'gifted, confident and skilled' etc.

Little do we comprehend; such people have undergone a time of preparation and refining through a 'fiery furnace' in their personal walk.

Neither do we consider whether we would opt for that journey had tables been turned around – to become the 'end-product' that we view in its finished state – the flamboyance! It is questionable.

They become part of the *circumstantial evidence to God's restorative power* -- He has redeemed them and they grow to know Him as the Rear Guard. He qualified them into eloquence, flamboyance.

We may oft overlook the process one went through – which 'qualifies them' into the 'effectiveness' in their conduct, outlook, fluency or special touch — and oft it's effectively their life story.

A story line of a journey – usually an extraordinarily '**pain-full**' journey extending over some years. This walk somewhat crafts them as God moulds them through the pain – and renders them as perceived – graciously effective and engaging, spirit-filled, comforting and nurturing— name it... in their nature.

Surprisingly these observations are not always common knowledge such individuals may have. They do not recognise the worth in themselves, but attribute all to the Master Himself who deserves all praise and acknowledgement. They know their Rear Guard.

They have learnt to recognise and accept God to be the rear guard... under difficult conditions; they adopt God's view of them and think less of themselves.

Lesson to take – it's in one's best interests to partner with God's perspective. Which oft represents God's perspective of them, and we become beneficiaries to God's completed work in them.

'Give thanks in all things, for it is His will for you' – this applies in ALL circumstances, though somewhat mankind appears to apply this scripture more to negative than positive circumstances.

Today- let's give thanks in ALL things.

Let's magnify anything positive which stands for how we're perceived through God's eyes;

While diminishing everything negative which partners with the enemy's devices and forces against us.

Experience is one of the best teachers — so is time. Perseverance is bred through Learning - to be steadfast in our faith and praise God in trials, with the knowledge that our hope does NOT disappoint, and we shall emerge triumphant.

"And not only that, but we also glory in tribulations, knowing that

Tribulation produces perseverance; ---, hope. Now hope does not disappoint, because The love of God has been poured out in our hearts. By the Holy Spirit who was given to us." (Romans 5)

Inspiration from God's word

"Faith Triumphs in Trouble:

Therefore, having been justified by faith,

We have peace with God through our

Lord Jesus Christ, through whom also

We have access by faith into this grace

In which we stand, and rejoice

In hope of the glory of God."

Prayer

Help us Lord to see You as our Rear Guard; And respect You as our Source of provision

We look to a Glorious & victorious day ahead. We proclaim it, and dare to live it - despite challenges ahead of us.

We Walk in spiritual victory, by faith and not by sight - help us focus on the target set before us.

Chapter 16

The Ultimate Prize

This - translates to living life on earth with a reframed mind-set to match the heavenly perspective of the spirit of adoption into 'sonship', as an heir to the throne along with Christ. (As we pray - 'Your Kingdom come... Your will be done, on earth as it is in heaven').

This perspective recognises the power we have in God, in shifting things from heaven to come into existence on earth - calling those things that are not in existence as though they were. And an anticipation of the reward, having fought a good fight of faith - that God will say; 'Well done - faithful servant'.

Quite often God's Heavenly Plan does not make earthly sense – usually not in the instant we expect Him to act. Mike Murdock intimates this as He shares some Godly wisdom.

I have been encouraged by the Anon Poet to the original 'Quilt of Holes' - presents an image of that desired affirmation from God. I oft draw strength from ending of the story below:

Quilt of Holes

As I faced my Maker at the last judgment, I knelt before the Lord along with all the other souls.

Before each of us laid our lives like the piles; an angel sat before each of us sewing our quilt squares together into a tapestry that is our life. But as my angel took each piece of cloth off the pile, I noticed how ragged and empty each of my squares was.

They were filled with giant holes. Each square was labelled with a part of my life that had been difficult, the challenges and temptations I was faced with in everyday life. I saw hardships that I endured, which were the largest holes of all. I glanced around me. Nobody else had such squares. Other than a tiny hole here and there, the other tapestries were filled with rich colour and the bright hues of worldly fortune.

I gazed upon my own life and was disheartened. My angel was sewing the ragged pieces of cloth together, threadbare and empty, like binding air.

Finally, the time came when each life was to be displayed, held up to the light, the scrutiny of truth. The others rose; each in turn, holding up their tapestries. So, filled their lives had been. My angel looked upon me, and nodded for me to rise. My gaze dropped to the ground in shame. I hadn't had all the earthly fortunes. I had love in my life, and laughter. But there had also been trials of illness, and wealth, and false accusations that took from me my world, as I knew it.

I had to start over many times. I often struggled with the temptation to quit, only to somehow muster the strength to pick up and begin again. I spent many nights on my knees in prayer, asking for help and guidance in my life. I had often been held up to ridicule, which I endured painfully, each time offering it up to the Father in hopes that I would not melt within my skin beneath the judgmental gaze of those who unfairly judged me.

And now, I had to face the truth. My life was what it was, and I had to accept it for what it was. I rose and slowly lifted the combined squares of my life to the light. An awe-filled gasp filled the air. I gazed around at the others who stared at me with wide eyes. Then, I looked upon the tapestry before me. Light flooded the many holes, creating an image, the face of Christ. Then our Lord stood before me, with warmth and love in His eyes.

He said, 'Every time you gave over your life to Me, it became My life, My hardships, and My struggles. Each point of light in your life is when you stepped aside and let Me shine through, until there was more of Me than there was of you.'

May all our quilts be threadbare and worn, allowing Christ to shine through! When there is nothing left but God that is when you find out that God is all you need.

It ends with a Prayer - which I'd encourage you to say for yourself too:

Father, God bless all my friends in whatever it is that you know they may need this day! And may their life be full of your peace, prosperity and power as they seek to have a closer relationship with you. Amen.

I was first made aware of this poem in 2008, when my closest friend couldn't find the right words to comfort me with anymore. I had gone through innumerable battles in my life. We walked a journey since university years -- she seemed to have always held this misconception that I was this strongest girl she met in her real life. We shared as much laughter in our joys as we shared tears. Tears came in form of pain and equally in an expression of inexplicable joy. We laughed a lot, the rolling-on the-floor type of laughter, lungs out and hurting from excessive exercise of the action!

This time, I appeared to have lost my joy. My smile disappeared.

I had been in a place where I felt choked, had goitre in the throat. I was in place of betrayal - serious betrayal, so deep by those I'd never have thought able to cause so much havoc in life. So deep was the pain that I'd not talk about it, no soul would comprehend. I talked to God, tears on my pillow each night for months on end. I was 'finished'. This journey, in which the attack laid, had been a lengthy walk - it took everything out of me. I felt worthless, and scared.

'Lord, could things have gotten any worse than they were?' I asked.

He led me to His very experiences recorded in Isaiah 53:7-8:

"He was oppressed and afflicted, yet he did not open his mouth; he was led like a lamb to the slaughter,

And as a sheep before its shearers is silent,

So he did not open his mouth.

By oppression and judgment he was taken away. Yet who of his generation protested?

For he was cut off from the land of the living;

For the transgression of my people he was punished.

He was despised and rejected by mankind, a man of suffering, and familiar with pain.

Like one from whom people hide their faces he was despised, and we held him in low esteem. Surely he took up our pain and bore our suffering, yet we considered him punished by God, stricken by him, and afflicted."

I had to believe this word after reading it on many nights when I cried myself to sleep – holding myself in foetal position and looking for comfort. That, was all God could give me at the time. Until it became reality in my life – I was no greater than Jesus, that knowledge sufficed over time.

I have read this poem numerous times, each time it resonates with my very experiences of life *of pain.*

My life has been full of pain of one form or another. But as I grew up, we had much joy in my home, so I struggled with my older years when simple things that made life funny and laughable and light-hearted jokes were becoming issues of contention as my world expanded. I struggled as I made efforts to shift my mode of operation and accommodate different modes of thinking, embracing others and loving them as I do.

The *Quilt of Holes* author must have had me in mind, or he was my double - in that they had as excruciating life experiences as mine... I pondered. I break into tears not for the hurt resurfacing, rather for the accuracy in presenting my experience so succinctly eloquently...

And God found a tangible way of communicating His thoughts to me. It reveals the life I've had to live and the endurance imposed by conditions that caused hurt. I tried to live for God through this - so that He may increase while I decrease. That His will prevailed in my life.

I have had to learn, particularly in the last two decades... to live life with a somewhat 'heavenly' eye-view, to maintain sanity and allow my pain to melt into the heart of God - as He hides me in the secret place of His tabernacle. There, I find safety. There I rest; there I find peace. There I feel warm, loved and embraced for only who I am. No conditions attached nor unrealistic expectations set against my continually failing nature that I wear my very human flesh.

I have, *as much as practically feasible within my limitations of human flesh,* tried to give way to God... albeit **'under duress**, imposed by storms of life...' as He enabled me - it's safer and serene to give way. I had no better or more appealing options within my hardships, than to let go and let God.

It had repeatedly proven an impossible journey to 'do life alone'. Constant insurmountable obstacles lay ahead since my 'real life' began in the phase of maturity in age.

As I pondered, another vivid recollection befell me, of similar experiences since the age of twelve-thirteen. I could not *survive* a day without reading the word of God to see me through, each night crying myself to sleep.

Being in boarding school far from home, I had to devise survival skills. I read 'where to find help from' sections of mini Gideon's bible laying under my pillow - to guide me to scripture and prayer so I could sleep. I was bullied through lies and framed stories that implicated me and defamed my character. I lost friendships that mattered to me, from the division created by the bullying. I could not protect myself, I had to focus and study hard and look to God, away from these distractors. I felt hated, of little worth. But God comforted me as life was made unbearable by my 'attackers'. I learnt to fully depend on Him.

As I was at nursery school aged four, my Mum had been in hospital for what seemed like a lifetime. My family would visit each evening - us altogether with my older siblings. My siblings would alternate staying with me by Mum's window outside her ward by a corner - holding me up to see her in view as we chatted the evening away. I was allowed into the ward for limited time being under age. Then after an hour or more we'd all congregate back into the car, heading home. The day, for me was made!

She had been bed bound till I was about nine-ten years old. As I was in high school, her illness appeared to creep in again and I'd never wanted her to keep suffering. I recall praying earnestly to God around those years, that I could understand - if that was God's plan – I would release her into heaven so that she found relief. This went on and off till I was at university when she became completely well. Wow, finally God healed her. I had left the horrible place in high school for a better institution at university. I could go home if push came to shove as my campus was within the city that my parents lived in. When similar experiences began to resurface (which did for a period), I could go home and refresh my mind. I began a new chapter of life. It would be different, God saw me through. After I completed my studies, I started work then married my husband Jonathan two years later – after seven years of courtship.

It only hit home that God saved my Mum for such times as these, when after our wedding, we had a car accident on the way to our honeymoon. I was incapacitated for a while; all my siblings were married off and there was no better nor more appropriate candidate while I also supported my husband then hospitalised; than my mum to move down to our house (we lived 20 minutes away from my family home) - to nurse me.

Further revelations have come over the years when I've needed her input in my life so desperately as I had children, that I would not imagine life without access to her.

This is an illustration only, of a painful life I'd greatly endured and prayed over... but results came only on God's terms -- His plan made sense only in my twenties until now, when the thought of access to her is comforting. As we speak, she's 82; strong enough to nurse my Dad who has severe dementia in his old age. Roles are switched... God knew she had to be here for her husband. We cannot even begin to imagine life without her... in the here and now. Nobody can nurse Dad and love him with the same commitment that she has. God had a plan I never foresaw. She humbly cares for Dad with such love as in serving her master without groaning - as in serving Christ.

"Do all things without complaining and disputing, that you may become blameless and harmless, children of God without fault in the midst of a crooked and perverse generation, among whom you shine as lights in the world, Holding fast the word of life, so that I may rejoice in the day of Christ that I have not run in vain or laboured in vain." (Philippians 2:14-16 NKJ)

Dared, once again - to trust Him

All these experiences ARE my life. It's not smooth. But I am happy enough and I trust God in it.

Can you trust Him... in the hallway, while it still hurts? My answer is yes. God gives us no temptation greater than what we can bear. In the end, all things work together for our good. *"No temptation has overtaken you except what is common to mankind. And God is faithful; he will not let you be tempted beyond what you can bear. But when you are tempted, he will also provide a way out so that you can endure it."* (1 Corinthians 10:13 – NIV)

Chapter 17

The Divine Design

It is a calling on our lives - as we are empowered by God, the Father through the Holy Spirit. Yet, the choice for ALL mankind to believe in His son Jesus for any benefits... is free. Free access, by choice.

One has access the benefits through Jesus as we are given the spirit of adoption into 'sonship', therefore we are heirs to the throne as we are intertwined and interlinked with God as is Jesus - by and in His love. Deeply routed by the completed work of the cross... so that resurrection power gives us a new dawn. We get and feel stronger as we operate in Him.

Whether in high places where God deserves ALL praise; or in low moments when He deserves your heart of worship; or indeed times that you feel alone and possibly lost - always remember that you are part of His Divine Design.

He wants a relationship with us, which will not be hindered by anything we do in our walk on planet earth. In fact, our walk is only in passing to the destination in heaven. However, God loves to see

His children impact on the world around them, so that the world too, may know Him through us.

In His creation of us in His image, He desired for us to be whole and to feel complete - it's His image we present and His character we represent.

'So God created mankind in his own image, in the image of God he created them; male and female he created them.' (Genesis 1:27)

He wants us to enjoy the inheritance He created and gave us to nurture. Let us maximise the benefits we hold as His divine design. There are no conditions - but acceptance of Him through Christ.

When faced with challenges we begin to doubt our worth, our inheritance, our self-image loses focus on the one who crafted us. These are times we ought to perceive ourselves as God does - through His lenses, in His image. More importantly, to cultivate and culture a habit of saying and claiming positive things over ourselves... meditating on the good excellent, noble, pure and praiseworthy things that reflect His image.

"Finally, brothers and sisters, whatever is true, whatever is noble, whatever is right, whatever is pure, whatever is

lovely, whatever is admirable – if anything is excellent or praiseworthy – think about such things." Philippians 4:8 NIV

It is crucial for us to recognise that His presence hangs about and hovers over us – that it is existent, for He says, 'I will be with you always'. Let us recognise this and remain in His presence, there we can conquer the world, enjoying the benefits stored up for us all, in His divine design. As His word proclaims:

"Then God said, 'Let us make mankind in our image, in our likeness, so that they may rule over the fish in the sea and the birds in the sky, over the livestock and all the wild animals, and over all the creatures that move along the ground.'" Genesis 1:26 NIVUK

"For if the inheritance depends on the law, then it no longer depends on the promise; but God in His grace gave it to Abraham through a promise." Galatians 3:18 NIV

Inspiration

If you're at that uncertain step in your journey...

You need to walk through to-day, to get to your designed destiny.

However hard today's challenge may seem,

Press on and get through --

Your blessing awaits, it fits your divine design.

May you find enough motivation through the expected end, to press in and press on?

"Begin with the end in mind."--TCASE 1st July '14

Prayer - Dwelling in His Presence

Father God, remind me to be aware of my divine design as a perfect reflection of your image. That I should remember to meditate on this about you:

'Basking in His presence is how all weakness dies,

Where the evil devices fail as God arises

Where the enemies scatter and run into confusion

What's paramount is magnifying Him,

For His kingdom to come down,

As His glory surrounds.' -- TCASE adaptation.

Chapter 18
The God of All Seasons

Indeed, it may sound like 'A Dare in The Face of Turmoil'! Yes, easier said than done.
No, not easy to put into practice.

But at times we have such limited options that, adopting such a strategy may be exactly what helps one to stay afloat. These are moments when you look around and you see no 'visible' helper in sight. No one appears to be stretching their hand toward you, to pull you out of the mire clay... the waters are rough, storms are ranging and winds are high - side to side - you look out for help; no one, none in sight to bail you out. The reality sinks in; you MUST keep fighting and swim against the waves, managing you breathing effectively. To keep your head held high – your chin up and forge forward. Eyes closed to somewhat miraculously cut through the raging seas -- in the hope that when you next open your eyes, you will have passed the worst. A slight hope remains – though options are limited. You must hold on to this level of faith, hope for victory. You do know victory is ahead if you keep moving forward.

You have a glimpse of hope in your heart of hearts, because *He who watches over you neither slumbers nor sleeps* {Psalm 121:4}.

That knowledge, the anticipation of the promise coming to pass - fuels you up and replenishes your depleted energy – He, God… won't let you down. Phew!

It is a morning of Friday, 03/02/17 and the Lord has brought back to my memory past things of my early childhood - ages 4/5 during kindergarten (nursery school) years into grade one of primary school.
I recall once when I had caught measles, Mummy was in her time away phases into hospital. It was a frustrating time as I had to miss school and stay home alone with my two companions - our pet dogs Cruiser and Daisy. I'd lay on a quilt in my veranda… by the corner we had a pair of single arm chairs and a mini table where Mum and Dad would have their evening tea. Early mornings and weekends when Mum was home, we'd all have brunch there, there used to be a beautiful sunflower and sunrise was a scenic view. Combined, the sunflower tilting its gaze to the sun provided an intriguing and breath-taking

view for a 4/5year old - right by our front garden. This was a comforting view and feel, such that in distress, sitting there provided some familiar cosiness

I reminisce over this time... that's where I'd be positioned on a quilt, relaxing and chatting to my pets while I waited for Victoria and Anthony to return from school at noon. This was before Stephen was co-opted into my family, as he joined us when I was in grade two. The waiting felt so long, that it helped me pass time to watch the sunflower tilting and dancing to the tune of the sunshine until it was upright... then I'd hear Dad's car approaching and my siblings would be arriving. Hooray!
Joy and relief would set in... my life would be complete again having my best friends by my side. We'd have lunch and then evenings back to full house. Repeating the pattern till I was clear of measles. God was always by my side, this now I realise.

I am the youngest in a family of 10 (two were adopted children - a sister via paternal uncle and a brother via maternal aunt). My parents were in the business of adopting and had the tendency to co-opt children into our family, from several of their extended families. This- was usually the first born of each household to offer them opportunities for education in the City. My parents emphasised that if our extended families in the village were provided with education, they would have eradicated to an extent – the level of poverty and hedged against our future so that these 'cousins, aunties, uncles etc... would not have to infinitely depend on us financially. Ok, whatever… (I was too young to pay attention, but I was happy with a home of **many** people! We laughed a lot.)

This translated into our family culture... I recall at one point there were twenty-one of us living in my home. To say I grew up like any other 'spoilt kids' being last born will therefore be far from the truth. Deeply loved, I was - spoilt I was NOT! I even had my own age-equivalent cousin, Stephen who became such a crucial part of me I'd never have wanted life without him. As my immediate older siblings were twins, Stephen effectively became my 'twin' too.

The Birthday Offering – 'Thank God for the mere gift of life': Mum

A vivid recollection of my early years includes sunny Saturday mornings when we would walk to church 12-15minutes away from my house. Our oldest siblings were in boarding high school or college and first two? working by then. With big brother Joe, one sister Voullista, the twins Victoria and Anthony plus myself, we would set off for church. Mum would join infrequently as she was oft in hospital. I recall though that she always gave us money to take to church for offering, and more importantly for our birthdays she gave us another special offering as thanks giving - for each to give to God in appreciation of the *gift of life*, that God had seen us through, to see THIS day. We did and birthday offering was special as, at junior church we would be asked to stand up and praise God, place offering in basket and thank him - on 'my' birthday... my special day. This habit has been embedded in me to this day. And I have learnt to treasure life in a particularly unique way on a birthday. It's a recognition that I learnt from Mum to make as a special gift: Life is extended. So, carrying this is a family value my Mum instilled in us – I always remember to *thank God for the mere gift of life*!

As I state, I rarely went to church with my Mum at this age. But she would remind my brother to give us a two penny each to give; on days that she came with us when I was older (seven-eight years old), she would give each of us the offering money. Birthday offering however, carried a new and different meaning, year in and year out. It was a special blessing from God and I needn't take it for granted. It has been even more profound as I have seen six of my older siblings miss this next birthday, or that next birthday.

As I write, it dawns on me all the more as reality sinks in. 'Thank God for the mere gift of life'... this year is different. My birthday approaches and it comes with mixed feelings as it falls due in two months. I am eager to get there so as to prove that God was, is and remains forever the Redeemer and Saviour of my life. The ultimate Living God who has given me hope in the absence of its physical existence.

The fact is... Of the ten children, my parents had, only three have made it to the age of fifty thus far. That – is a very low statistic. As of now (Feb 2017) only 30% made it to the age of 50! The rest died well before - with my first-born sister missing her 50th by only six months, in Feb 2002.

Guess what, I am the next one taking up this challenge. Question is -- will I make fifty? 'Lord', I ask Abba Father... how did this happen – they died at a premature age, even cousin Stephen - my 'twin did not come this far. My brother Tony didn't even make 40, he was only 39 and Victoria was 46. These were my companions and play mates. Every heartfelt childhood memory I hold has these three deeply linked or tightly attached to'... my questioning continues until I burst out into tears.

Then God reminds me once again, that He is a God of all seasons. And what I write today will be a testimony for my 50th birthday. 'How will I, oh God'...? I'm in tears and wonder, when He warms my heart with a gentle touch - a faint smile on my face, a subtle expression of joy emerges in my heart. Sufficient to bring real laughter. But my emotions are too broken for laughter... so I gently smile. Sobbing away and walking into His embrace.

But the message I take with me is that, I will 'see' fifty. God assures me and I must simply believe and prepare the testimony. It's about His faithfulness and His glory not about me per se. Rather He will display His splendour through me as I flourish in Him. As I allow myself to swim in an avalanche of His endearing love and savour His tenderness. Yet, I feel so inadequate and imperfect through my questioning. I don't consider myself worthy and anointed sufficiently to display this, His splendour.

"See, I am doing a new thing! Now it springs up; do you not perceive it? I am making a way in the wilderness and streams in the wasteland." (Isaiah 43:19 - NIV)

A standard of grace and not perfection

God reminds me two days later that as His vessel, He holds me to standard of grace and not perfection. That I am the imperfect vessel perfected by His love and sanctified by the blood of Jesus hence qualified by grace as His WORTHY VESSEL.

That reduces me to my knees. Internally... I can only stand in awe of Him. A faint smile on my face. I am of value. Something of true value to God and that suffices for the here and now. He is dealing with me, hushing and pacifying me in my distress and brokenness. He does so while imploring me to drop many beliefs and attitudes that I hold but do not align with Him nor represent His truth. To drop the perfectionism and embrace His grace; drop self-righteousness, drop self-sufficiency to wholly depend on Him, and drop man's opinion of me by recognising that I am qualified by grace. To drop any worry or judgements of my very self.

He positions me in the place of 'DROPPINGS'. Training me to consistently and intentionally drop any guilt and embrace freedom, drop condemnation and embrace acceptance, drop fear and embrace power and sound mind, drop rejection and embrace sonship where we cry out Abba Father. Drop all negative things that have fed into my thinking and my life and step higher into His grace and greater heights as He redeems us into Royal priesthood. I hold at my disposal unmerited favour and reflect God's character through righteousness by sanctification. Justification by faith in Him. By faith as Abraham was dealt with. Hallelujah.

Romans 4:13 and 16 (NLT) affirms our position in God:

"Clearly, God's promise to give the whole earth to Abraham and his descendants was based not on his obedience to God's law, but on a right relationship with God that comes by faith."

"So the promise is received by faith.
It is given as a free gift. And we are all certain to receive it, whether or not we live according to the law of Moses, if we have faith like Abraham's.
For Abraham is the father of all who believe.

Hebrews 11:8 & 17 (NLT) state:
"It was by faith that Abraham obeyed when God called him to leave home and go to another land that God would give

him as his inheritance. He went without knowing where he was going.

It was by faith that Abraham offered Isaac as a sacrifice when God was testing him. Abraham, who had received God's promises, was ready to sacrifice his only son, Isaac," Trust that the God Who creates, who makes, who provides and redeems – will also deliver on His promises as He fights for you; even though your experiences may suggest otherwise.

"For you shall not go out with haste, nor go by flight; For the Lord, will go before you, and the God of Israel will be your rear guard." Isaiah 52:12

This is when we realise that in the good times or bad, Jesus is always alive... and because He lives, we can face tomorrow. We dare to lay our lives in His hands. One of my latest experiences has revealed God's character imbued in me. I have had a difficult few weeks and have been sustained by Him to get through to the end of one crucial journey - just before getting to a breaking point.

Having been in isolation but constant communion with Abba Father in the season, I was at a point of utter exhaustion; and had few circles to pray with me.

The severity symptoms of the temporary illness I fall into at times had been alleviated by the power of God. As I explained briefly, in Feb - April 2013 or so I suffered intermittent paralysis on the right, unable to care for myself nor walk. I fought with the word and in offensive prayer against the enemy to overcome. Whom you see today is already a testimony of God's truth.

While unwell, I received and still do as He reminds me... messages that at times we must take time to rest. I've been having that rest and the Lord has fed me endlessly in His own way, almost intentionally separated from activity for His purpose.

"Count it all joy when you go through trials... consider it all joy..." James 1:1-3

This is yet another testimony to come to pass. I learn to take heart, be at peace amidst the storm... a season that is passing.

We harbour pain and suffering at times and through that, we still minister to others and in that experience

- we display the power of Christ at work through us - not by mere choice to suffer, but a source of comfort in spite the suffering. God assures us we are covered in grace:

"But he said to me, "My grace is sufficient for you, for my power is made perfect in weakness."

"Therefore I will boast all the more gladly about my weaknesses, so that Christ's power may rest on me." (2 Corinthians 12:9 - NIV

"Each time he said, "My grace is all you need. My power works best in weakness."

- So now I am glad to boast about my weaknesses, so that the power of Christ can work through me." (NLT)

My current challenge remains in our daughter's illness as well as my own in recent years. Managing self... then working, being an effective Mum as well as remaining a functional wife, friend and whatever other capacity I serve in for other relations has proved a challenge.

I know God is with me always - it is the truth and it remains - Jesus lives in me.

The simple question still resurfaces at intervals: where is God in my suffering, where is God in my illness, where is God in --- I could go on and on but reality remains as I hold the knowledge that the Redeemer lives.

"I know that my redeemer lives, and that in the end he will stand on the earth. And after my skin has been destroyed, yet in my flesh I will see God; I will see him with my own eyes – I, and not another. How my heart yearns within me!" (Job 19:25-27)

He is God in the infirmity, He is God in my strength, and He is God. Come rain or shine... noon time or night, sowing time and in harvest, He is God in the moonlight or sunshine -- He is God in every situation...

In fact, He is a God of ALL seasons. He was God before the moonlight and after the sunshine... He was God before creation and after... He is God regardless of my physical limitations and any circumstances. He is the eternal God from yesterday to Infinity. Simple, no argument.

Scripture reminds us, that we ought to glorify God even in our weakness, in the storm, in all trials. I must glorify Him in all situations, in and out of season. Romans 5:3 challenges me:

"And not only that,

But we also glory in tribulations, knowing that tribulation produces perseverance; - and perseverance, character; and character, hope. Now hope does not disappoint, ---
Because the love of God has been poured out in our hearts by the Holy Spirit who was given to us." (Rom 5:3)

Can we fit the Calling - loving the broken into wholeness?

Similarly, when people instead of ourselves are in dire suffering, we learn to love them by being emphatic. We learn to accept them in their weakness which may include 'ill-behavioural displays' - but Christ has exemplified in His years of ministry that He separated the behaviour and the actions from the person and looked beyond them. Which meant He'd have no other option but to love, love that human being no matter how 'unlovable' they look in our eyes. Until they became whole.

Can we fit the Calling? Can we love people out of their brokenness into wholeness? God expects us to *love people into wholeness.* Rebuild them through loving them unconditionally. Displaying the agape love.

In Matthew 26:7 We hear the story of Mary Magdalene, the Alabaster box... she used her expensive perfume to anoint Jesus, it was her sacrifice and expression of an endearing love that she'd been shown while she was yet a sinner. She had to minister back to Him after He had shown her the non-judgemental, agape' love – in spite of her faults, and brought her back into wholeness: *"While he was eating, a woman came in with a beautiful alabaster jar of expensive perfume and poured it over his head".* (NLT)

One of the three women to see Jesus first after resurrection was Joanna. Joanna, wife of Chuza is believed to have been one of Jesus' disciples during the time of His ministry - though women were not readily identified as disciples. She was a hospitable woman who gave her service through her substance. By virtue of being a wife to Herod's manager, she capitalised on her position to access many of Herod's workers and share the gospel of Jesus with them. This was a divine positioning as inferred in biblical commentaries, that it was effectively 'VIP' access she had in Herod's home. She obtained mercy to be able to minister to the workers.

"Joanna, the wife of Chuza, Herod's business manager; Susanna; and many others who were contributing from their own resources to support Jesus and his disciples". Luke 8:3 NLT

We read of her ministry, indicative of the financial responsibility she took over Jesus and His disciples. She paid for upkeep - what we would consider hotel accommodation, catering and related needs for the Lord and His disciples wherever they travelled. She's believed to have been rich, materially. But guess what, she gave from the fullness of her heart, her bosom into which Jesus made deposits by loving her into wholeness. He healed her infirmity and she became loyal to Him.

We wonder why we don't always bring souls to Christ... well, we place loads and piles of judgments on them and then condemn them. By inference through our actions, they believe we present God's spirit of condemnation - so, they run! They run from Him due to our misrepresentation of who God is. For them, they should see God as love which was *'given to me while I was yet a sinner'* (Romans 5:8).

If I love God with my heart, I must express this too. He's a God of 'Agape love'. When I'm in sin am out of season, when am righteous am in season... and He is God either way. The difference is He sanctified me into righteousness when I received Him. The season for me changes, on the other hand *God is the constant* that never changes. I am work-in-progress - to reflect God's agape love. Not many would reject God if we present this fact and reality, accurately to them? Food for thought...

A dare to trust!

'Dare to trust. Dare to persevere. Dare to hold your peace!

He promises, Behold, I make all things new.

"Then your light shall break forth like the morning, your healing shall spring forth speedily, and your righteousness shall go before you; the glory of the Lord shall be your rear guard.

Then you shall call, and the Lord will answer; you shall cry, and He will say, 'Here I am.' "If you take away the yoke from your midst, the pointing of the finger, and speaking wickedness..." (Isaiah 58 excerpt)

Remember, God fights your battles and you shall hold your peace in the time of battle.

"You will keep in perfect peace, those whose minds are steadfast because they trust in you." (Isaiah 26:3). You're blessed in your coming in and going out...

Sometimes God is only propelling you to start stepping out of your comfort zone and we need to be open-minded to perceive these moments as blessings in disguise. He appoints us for specific assignments and part of the process may be going through testing in a refinery.

The song 'Blessings' by Laura Story reminds me to embrace my situation at each point of difficulty, in reminding me that God's blessings sometimes come in different forms from what we expect. Consider how rain counts as a blessing in the face of drought. This means that if rains poured so heavily that floods also arose, we would not immediately 'curse' the rain due to flooding. We would acknowledge the rain that watered the land and then plead with God to contain the rain. It would not be ALL bad news.

Similarly, excessive sun shine without any raindrops causes drought and whirlwind or wild fires. While we would need the sun to dry flooding fields, if the drying exceeded the contained limits, it would defeat the very purpose which we prayed for the weather change.

It is question of seeing things in context. Laura story illustrates these mixed feelings of conflicting situations in life. Because sometimes, the trials of this life, are God's mercies but disguised.

'Cause what if your blessings come through raindrops; What if Your healing comes through tears; What if a thousand sleepless nights are what it takes to know you're near...

What if my greatest disappointments, Or the aching of this life.

Is the '*Revealing of a greater thirst, this world can't satisfy'*.

And what if trials of this life: The rain, the storms, the hardest nights

Are your mercies in disguise..."?

Inspiration

Whether in high place or the lows of this life...
God will bless your coming in & going out. Remember:
"Basking in His presence
Is how all weakness dies?
Where the evil devices fail
God arises while His enemies scatter
What's paramount is magnifying Him
As His glory surrounds."

Be in the zone! Decree it. Declare it. Receive it. For His glory to manifest in our midst.

Blessings - Laura Story: Full Lyrics

We pray for blessings. We pray for peace
Comfort for family, protection while we sleep
We pray for healing, for prosperity
We pray for your mighty hand
To ease our suffering. All the while,
You hear each spoken need
Yet love is way too much to give us lesser things

<u>Bridge</u>
'Cause what if your blessings come through raindrops
What if Your healing comes through tears
What if a thousand sleepless nights are what it takes to know You're near
What if trials of this life are Your mercies in disguise

We pray for wisdom, Your voice to hear
We cry in anger when we cannot feel You near
We doubt your goodness, we doubt your love
As if every promise from Your Word is not enough
All the while -- You hear each desperate plea
And long that we'd have faith to believe

When friends betray us
When darkness seems to win
We know the pain reminds this heart
That this is not, this is not our home
It's not our home
«« Bridge »»
What if my greatest disappointments
Or the aching of this life
Is the revealing of a greater thirst,
this world can't satisfy. And what if trials of this life
The rain, the storms, the hardest nights
Are Your mercies in disguise.

All in all, God's grace has been the sustaining power behind my survival.

Times have been hard and times have been challenging enough to throw me into a place where I lost hope.
I can say with God I have defeated negative thoughts in most trying times and applied God's word as instructed

In 2 Corinthians 10:5
"We demolish arguments and every pretension that sets itself up against the knowledge of God, and we take captive every thought to make it obedient to Christ." NIV
"We destroy every proud obstacle that keeps people from knowing God. We capture their rebellious thoughts and teach them to obey Christ." (NLT)

The love of God has somewhat filled some of the vacuum created by losses I have suffered and pain I have endured to a point that I am able to share the stories in which the hurts have been overridden by God's perspective of personal worth and my value to Him -- through His lenses.

This epitomises the reward of embracing the resurrection power that Jesus Christ offers to us. Bringing us into wholeness in spite of life's difficulties - bearing witness to the benefits arising from the completed work of the cross.

The reality is, God's ways are higher than ours - and in one form, or other the above needs are being met and vacuum filled individually - through God's crafted ways by the shifting of things in the heavenly realm.

"For my thoughts are not your thoughts, neither are your ways my ways," declares the LORD.

"As the heavens are higher than the earth, so are my ways higher than your ways and my thoughts than your thoughts--"!

To God be ALL honour and glory, in Christ Jesus.

My prayer is that you are enabled to keep forging forward and feel equipped.

Access via online support is available as needs arise.

Links to a Facebook page 'The chaise a serenity escape' and Web are in appendices.

Be blessed. Be watered. Be rejuvenated in accepting God's hand to walk you the journey.

Every blessing and Agape' love!

In His Service,

Pao.
Xo!

Pao Viola Mbewe (Nee: Jedegwa)

Final Remarks

Special Acknowledgements in full

NB: By the time of publication, Dad has passed on to heaven – RIP on 4th April 17.

To serve as a tribute to Dad and Mummy - Benson Vasco Jim and Bessie Flossie Jedegwa, at a crucial stage of my Dad's life.

A recognition in honour of my Dad who is now 95, frail and feeble. I pray that he can receive and listen to this content as Mum would read to him; before he shifts into heaven to his Master. And honour my family – having lost so many siblings that I cannot take life for granted. I will therefore register sentiments when they are present to hear them – otherwise, the price is too high.

My parents, for endearing love, guidance and discipline.

Dad, your firm ways and admirable work ethic left nothing to be desired, a mark, and a thumb-print I have been shaped to emulate. I have embedded discipline and self-management skills, great initiative and deliver in different settings.

You challenged me, from an early age reminding me to be a reader-- our Chimbiza library you built over your years of study from St Francis Xavier university, to your further studies as you worked in Zambia with Mummy and your boys; to your continual studies while in long-term service with ADMARC into the capacity of a Regional Marketing Accountant before your retirement - all shaped the woman I have become.

Your involvement in partnering with Mum on how we dressed and stepped of our home was not acknowledged till later in my life -- you're a man! But made sense when I recall that you used to be the chairman of the Malawi Beauty Pageant. My big brothers adopted these positive traits, we didn't step out the house looking half presentable - we carried your name hence portrayed the 'family image' in our conduct.

You questioned me after I took university options to study accountancy-- I made no provision for a backup course -- only ticked 'Accountancy' for options 1,2&3. I was that certain of my aspirations. You questioned my commitment as you stated you were in the career and I observed the numerous nights you worked late at home, knocked off late and oft on weekends.

You made me rethink this -- it would be my life as it was a challenging course not only to study, but also has continued high demands on one's delivery. Once I registered my certainty, you empowered me to succeed. We shared study times together, as you worked late, you gave me tuition when some subjects were tough. I felt empowered for believing in me. Then you implied upon my graduation, that I could continue studying to attain the highest possible qualification and reach my highest potential. I knew you were not bound by cultural beliefs - a woman could be propelled into higher education and levels of success in our world.

I have delivered as best as able - despite delays in balancing family with my career. Except I have not yet visited your university in Canada, which has remained on your wish list.

I promise I will, as I wait in hope that there will be a provision at God's appointed time to enable deliver this. Whether you live to witness this is God's issue - as you're now 95. But I will continue to write and research.

You and Mum have called me a 'Joseph' of the family on numerous occasions when I doubted my position in stepping in to bail out situations at home. You gave me a voice when I believed I was 'too small'. That empowered me as I believe you prophetically spoke over my life. I have humbly taken my tasks on and graciously delivered - from the grace of God and nurturing in which you and Mum have clothed me; as well as the buffers in which my older siblings cushioned me. I could never ask for more.

To Mummy, *the ultimate role model - the first person I watched and admired as she relentlessly displayed the qualities and traits of a virtuous and mighty woman of valour in the way she executed her role as the effective mother and wife, big sister, an Aunt, a cousin, a friend, a political figure in capacity of vice chairman in the women's association for a local forum / branch - amidst numerous challenges thrown her way - which I only learnt much about via my siblings in my university years. Strength, determination, the joy of the Lord, kingdom focus and a forgiving spirit, describe the woman who raised me in the highs and lows of her life. I live today following your footsteps, reading the word and singing praises and worship before bedtime (with a cuppa in hand, of course) and in moments of distress, and praying for my husband and children plus wider support network because I 'watched' you do this day in, day out - come rain or shine. You were exemplary in your gracious conduct. Save for those numerous moments with an expression of joy in them, I do not recollect ever seeing you in visible distress or in tears --of pain. Yet the life that I've learnt you endured at times, would break any ordinary woman. You're extraordinary - I pray to follow in and live out that legacy beyond my generational - empowering the future generations.*

Your partnership with Dad in raising us with high standards of education, has impacted my life.

You delivered high class. It was apparent when you were out of action in hospital because meals were a little substandard. While big sister Eve was in college, my brothers would then step in to cook. They emulated you, showed how well you trained your boys - to be reliable, self-reliant and excellent even in the kitchen – zones defined as exclusive for females. A westernised view but you looked more to empowering your sons, having had three consecutively after your first daughter who was in boarding school - leaving the boys to fend for themselves. You equipped them, I felt safe under their care when you spent months on end, in hospital. I was only four, then five, six and then…nine

My brothers: *Frank - for providing for our physical needs every birthday in Mum's absence while Dad was busy with work. I still recall going into Mummy's bedroom to find you'd laid for each of us a set of special clothes, sets of socks and matching accessories labelled with days of a full week... Tears break to know I could never tell you this* ***again****, that learning days of the week was fun - but you hear me from heaven.*

Vyson - your endearing love and care, taking your lesson breaks from high school to come home and make dinner, laying for us to eat in good time as Mummy was in hospital -- no greater love than this. It wasn't a mere obligation, you provided for Voullista, Victoria, Anthony

Victor and I, a safe and secure environment in most challenging circumstances when you were studying for university.

We felt covered by your embrace. The provision while in high school, and direction on how to study, setting ambitious standards for education and guidance on techniques to excel - through to university years all moulded me into the accomplished woman I am today. Accomplishment in my eyes... is defined by personal enrichment and contentment in spirit and humanity, topped by excellence and integrity on a professional platform - not financial and material worth - I have that success. The level of selflessness you displayed over years, is admirable.

Joe - in inexplicably numerous selflessness ways, consistently and constantly flowing - you cared and loved, smiled to wipe my lonely tears away... warm embraces and ensuring I lacked completely nothing. This made me feel significant, not only loved. I mattered, we little ones being home without Mum around as she lay in a hospital bed - mattered and you looked over your shoulder to see if you had to go... that we were fine, ok and safe. Your protection still presents now, at times annoyingly as you remain over-protective (sorry, I've to add that - I'm 49!!). I know All this comes with love and has been for my best interests.

Anthony - God gave me a brother and sister that became my best friends. I can never begin to explain how fulfilled I always was. I still have letters you wrote me at university, I read them. I feel empty in your absence. It's tangible, the vacuum remains.

***My sisters**, Evelyn and Voullista - your partnership in mothering me has created safety, all my life. Pocket money and goodies were never running low. University years saw a closeness and bond stronger than I would have imagined - advice on being a big girl, provision and direction gave me confidence as I blossomed into a woman. Your affirmation made me secure. Voullie, you remain this strong support- long after Eve shifted into heavenly places.*

Victoria - my other self - I am because you were; as I know that you became who you were, because I was who I am. Life without you is a price that I continue to pay for deep love – pain, grief. But Jesus lives in me, so I can face tomorrow. I await our reunion.

I treasure you all, indescribably.

You gave me so much joy, security, love and laughter through continually flowing jokes in our home... that I grew up feeling whole and content. My children know how much you sowed into my life. That you love them too.

P.s: Frank/Vyson/Joe (&Mike) - I hold a vivid recollection of our 'movie date' at the Apollo cinema, and made me eat as much ice cream as I craved for. Shockingly you bought so much of it to finish before movie was screening - that I had to surrender - 'hands up', defeated. You made your point; I needed to stop demanding ice cream all the times you appeared... a lesson learnt, bittersweet experience for a pre-teen. I now think you mistook me for a toy... :) Thank you!

You created such buffers around me that I grew in confidence and contentment. So much that I have developed survival strategies in difficulties knowing I can achieve, inbuilt resilience deriving from complete and unconditional love you lavished me with carries me through.

May God honour you - Vyson, Joe and Voullie - my living siblings.

In absentia - I pray God Continues to heal my brokenness in His mercy as I strive to walk in His grace, for His glory and reunite with you: Evelyn Verlin, Vivian Ness, Frank Vinga, Mike Masautso, Victoria Jean and Anthony Victor - my physically absent siblings.

My heart remains sore but God shields it and wraps me in the robe of righteousness - Jesus covers my heart in the soft linen for protection. His resurrection power giving me hope... for death lost its sting. The grave was defeated by the Resurrection King.

To my husband, Jonathan.

For remaining by my side and enabling me to achieve everything I set out to do. We had a dare for each other when we met at university -

'...even if you don't get accepted - just go and prove yourself; even if it doesn't work out... just go and prove yourself. I recall playing this dare on you for the job that took us out of Malawi beyond our borders... 'I don't think I can live away from Malawi, we are getting married in two months and I won't have adjusted let alone cope with living away from my family... But, just go and prove yourself!' I intimated.

Proving ourselves has seen us progress into this station, station now in UK. With your passion taking you beyond the UK to Europe, East Asia, The Caribbean, Southern and Central Africa, Sub-Saharan African countries... while our daughter's and I keep the home front running; and we continue to challenge ourselves to excel for the betterment of self.

Thank you for believing that I can deliver and letting me get on with it but being on hand and accessible.

My children - the constant and at times uninvited cheerleaders! 'Mum you can do this, Mum that's so you, Mum if you don't - then who will. This fits your cut, or it's your second nature' - and more...! Well, no pressure - you've spelt an absence of doubt which is humbling.

Thank you, you have all been an anchor in my life

Immense love and divine guidance.

Prayers and Resources

From my heart - in desperation and as **an expression of God's love for comfort when in need.**

Gratitude and thanksgiving – to draw inspiration from and I offer my appreciation for the readers

Much appreciation for support and keeping things in place. While looking to venturing into next steps.

To thoughtful you, from thankful me.

Much gratitude for being positioned where you are

Looking to water the Lord's field when the brook dries up.

Just singing praise and adoration to the Lord who loves us unconditionally, that He has sustained us through storms and given us moments of laughter and a sense of contentment in life. We have seen sunshine through each other's eyes even when the waves have been high.

Sometimes a mere thought of you - a visual of your face... each one individually - brings a smile 'in my heart'.

So, this is taking the opportunity to give thanks to God for being you, and allowing Him to use you as His instruments to touch a life in time of need and share joys in happy times. Such sweet fellowship is an honour and a treasure.

My prayer is that as he refines you, He refreshes you all with running rivers and restores health where restoration is needed. That divine protection, health, security, safety and significance be your portion in this life from today forwards - as we drink of His fountain of love.

For the Lord cometh to give life in abundance, satisfy with long life and grant peace as His Father gives it.

Remain conquerors of this world - for He watches over His word in order to perform it.

You're always at heart and in prayer as prompted.

Much love & blessings

Enjoy the last of sunshine...

X

"I thank the Lord at every remembrance of you...

And this is my prayer: that your love may abound more and more in knowledge and depth of insight,

10 so that you may be able to discern what is best and may be pure and blameless for the day of Christ, filled with the fruit of righteousness that comes through Jesus Christ – to the glory and praise of God." Phil 1:3-6/7--

Divine Design - the 'envisioned snippets' library

Some experiences the Lord has given and I was unsure whether real or I envisioned in my soul.

If these may encourage only one soul, for God's glory will transcend.

Petitions and Results

Following a cry over health battles - vision I saw:

'It is now well... hold your peace. God has taken over'.

Am giving praise and keeping you covered to remain still in spirit despite physical pain of status quo.

The spiritual realm is released open - no limits just seamless sort of cloud appearance.

I see an expanse of....

Openness... a vast bright yellow-ish tones.

a seamless expanse with no end, an image of sort of brightness, gentle sunshine across that expanse. No dividing rays... just as would seem in a cloud view - but it's colours are variations of yellow.

God's precious child lays in an open room in her bed... there are no walls but it feels as though she still has these seers (beings kind of... keeping a casual distant - not intense - eye on her....)

She's seemingly peaceful with no worry, no visible excitement per se - rather a stillness and sense of contentment about her... she's comfortable... (I'm in tears) --- usually that happens when God's presence surrounds...

God's precious daughter is still upward looking as she lays in her bed as though in anticipation of the 'descending messiah from clouds - as she gazes up there she displays an aura of joy, freedom and she is simply content with her life despite the status-quo.

I sense as though she has a connection with her Father, her Creator hence the stillness in sort of awaiting... hand holding so she can 'come along'... there, where the expanse appears...

Visualise a cloud but in yellow colours of the sun without a dazzle / nor glare... just soft smooth colours as would be of clouds...

This is a God given image of a child He so loved. I give thanks for eternity with them.

As God's design for His child's life – He was faithful to reconcile the child back to Himself.

=====================================

Support and Inspiration Access Link

Birth of The Chaise. An Escape into Serenity

(http://thechaiseaserenityescape.wordpress.com/)

This journey progressed into a Facebook Page viz 'thechaiseaserenityescape'

Eventually a blog via free Web - WordPress.com access - being birthed in June 2014. With the intention to collate some inspirational thoughts and prayers as I'd write to self or to close friends in needs, over past years. To draw them onto a single access point.

About the page - Purpose of the Chaise a Serenity Escape

Design to 'Embark' on a journey while praying that God creates in us a passion; to be His instrument of peace and walk through life's 'streets & storms' - exuding His love.

As we know, it is a guarantee that life hands one insurmountable obstacles at one point or another in their journey on planet earth.

The resultant unspoken hurts, 'invisible' existence or being in an 'incognito state' oft being the harsh reality for some. Others may feel forgotten.

The Chaise is a virtual escape to a place of serenity, away from the noise, pain and busyness of this life.

It depicts a 'chill corner' for anyone desiring a break, to offload a burden, share, shed a tear, laugh, converse, or indeed sit in silence and just be... in virtual fellowship. It is a simple community outreach.

An opportunity for those weighed down, the youth in particular - to come, sit still, chill and relax, away from the heavy traffic of a busy world with its storms.

The Chaise offers an escape from life's harsh reality, into a moment of stillness and reflection, accessing positive tools to help one rise above challenging situations.

Therefore, participation would be welcome -- to share and receive, deposit into spiritual and emotional bank accounts; at any point of need - with open access to all as they feel liberated to do so. Offering a sense of 'Immense peace and Agape' love' - no premonitions, preconceptions or judgements attached.

=====================================

Links to encouraging messages encountered and music accesses at the time of writing this book:

https://www.psychologytoday.com/blog/career-transitions/200902/rejection-the-hell-in-the-hallway:

Katharine Brooks Ed.D. - Career Transitions

https://www.youtube.com/watch?v=D0BUFR9wSko - 0:12 / 25:50: Brad Jersak - The Gospel in Chairs

http://www.patheos.com/blogs/christiancrier/2014/11/12/what-does-it-mean-to-be-seated-with-christ-in-the-heavenly-places/ - Heavenly places

http://biblehub.com/matthew/26-7.htm - Joanna's ministry

Glossary

a. *Absent father* - In Moynihan's (1965) 'pathology of the matriarchy' hypothesis stated that the absence of a father is destructive to children because it means that they will lack the economic resources, role models, discipline, structure and guidance that a father provides.
(https://thepsychologist.bps.org.uk/volume-23/edition-10/fathers-behaviours-and-childrens-problems)

For the purposes of this book, 'absent fathers' refers to any form of guardian who is an influential parental figure in one's life and upbringing - both male and female

The subject is also inspired by a profound teaching received in 2008: Absent Fathers by Dr Mark Stibbe - Father's House Trust.

(https://www.thefreelibrary.com/Absent+fathers%3A+effects+on+abandoned+sons.-a020869562)

b. *Heavenly places* – Signifies a place of spiritual abode as 'Paul says that we are already seated with Christ in the heavenly places' in Ephesians 1:3-4 - "Blessed be the God and Father of our Lord Jesus Christ, who has blessed us in Christ with every spiritual blessing in the heavenly places, - even as he chose us in him before the foundation of the world, that we should be holy and blameless before him."

"...Now we are told that we are seated "with him in the heavenly places" meaning that, like Christ, our works are done. We are not saved by works but saved for works - but our works had nothing to do with our being saved. That's why we are as good as in heaven already and we are essentially already seated there with Christ because God sees things that are not yet as though they already are because in His mind, they are!"

(http://www.patheos.com/blogs/christiancrier/2014/11/12/what-does-it-mean-to-be-seated-with-christ-in-the-heavenly-places/ -260217)

c. *Hallway of pain* - The phase between the storm and a place of restoration and victory (time-span in *waiting between a closed door and the next open door*).

d. *Orphaned heart* – Kingdom Life definition: 'one who has been deprived of a parent or parents by either death or desertion. In the Greek, the term is *orphanos* and is translated parentless, fatherless, and comfortless. It figuratively speaks of one who is bereft of a teacher, guide, or guardian...orphan heart is a learned behaviour that becomes entrenched in the internal paradigm or mind-set. The source of this is deep wounding that most commonly occurs from the father. These deep wounds release a host of emotions in the soul that ultimately separates the child from the identity, security, sense of destiny, and purpose that, by design, are to be instilled by the father.'

(http://kingdomlife.org/the-orphan-heart-defined/ - 260217)

e. *'Rough and tough' of life* – In the context of this book, the process of daily living which presents such continual difficulties that survival mode becomes one's resolution in 'doing life' - getting by with enormous struggle

f. *Offering of praise as my Sacrifice* – The act of honouring God with your substance

g. *Divine Design* – The person who God created you to become – with your purpose

h. *TCASE - "The Chaise - A Serenity Escape"*: the author's Facebook page (thechaiseaserenityescape) and Blog (thechaiseaserenityescape.wordpress.com).

i. *TKCC* - The Kings Church Chesham - the author's current local church.

A Poem: When My Hero Goes To Sleep

Tribute to Dad on 06.04.17 - RIEP

Fare Ye Well Daddy:

No emotion... yet, flat, plain sense-full and tasteless feel... spreads across the room

No fragrance... no identifiable sensation...

But a tangible... sense of 'lost-lessness'

The lost sheep... no guide? No shepherd!?

I run..., like a sheep..., a lamb would run ahead, right ahead where a slim ghastly light fed through

Into that expanse... beautiful, but fading...

Fading into a silent, yet serene attractive endless seam.... it faded into a narrowing arrow possible ending.

This lamb..., paused, stopping for a minute to check over her shoulder.

See..., who else is coming in the distance? Who else comes with me on my journey,

Following this attractive beam of light

That projects into a myriad of dazzling rays of rainbow, Yet fading...

Is anyone coming along!?

The voice, her voice... the lamb's voice was heard in the echoes in that expanse...

The echoes repeated... loud, getting consumed into the wide expanse!

Echo… echo… echo..., Echoes…? Why...?

Oohhh... she run... she run further forwards to her hero, she run - to catch him

She run to catch up with him and hold his hand.

But something, something today is different... huh... huh... (the lamb panting)

Hold his hand... he always extends his hand

To hold mine... c'mon!

Mummy, Mummy, Mummy…

Why don't you come, Mummy...?

'Am I lost…?'

No-no, no my girl… you're not lost

No, my girl... not lost.

Dad left on the day you told us, told him…

That you're a grown up

That… you're a big girl, that you're now… 50

Dad went to unite with grandpa & granny,

And your other siblings

Because… now you said… you're a big girl

Now you said that, You can look after Mummy

Now you said… everyone will be safe…

Remember, you're his Joseph.

Now is the time he wants you to look after

The nations… go on, go on my girl.

Go on, it's ok. God's guiding light…

Will show you the way,

Jesus, will light the way… See

Your old woman needs you now; -- your hand.

OK, Mummy. *Finally, the penny dropped!*

The lamb... in a gentle walk.. in a slow amble walk...

She looks back... over her shoulder; she returns, she follows Mummy -- waiting on the far end.

Where she, waited patiently for her to find out for herself. That she... grew up.

They hold hands… time to save the nation...

She says... Okay.

'Daddy - sleep well - in God's loving arms.

With Mum, you both taught us class, excellence and grace, most importantly... to love ALL mankind.

Miss you, yes... yet you're only absent, and not missing. That's our comfort!

Sleep well… The Hero of this, my world.'

For **Benson Vasco Jim Jedegwa (BVJ)**

To depict his passions for reading and writing

To eradicate ignorance and poverty

from within our very beginnings.

A Poem - 'When My Hero Goes To Sleep'

A special dedication - describes her vision

By: Pao Jedegwa Mbewe (a.ka. 'Anapao Ananyada')

Fondly Known to her Daddy as *'Khombwani'* - in Sena

Meaning *'the baby of the house'*

Rest In Eternal Peace – 6th April, 2017.

Notes and Inner Thoughts